LOSING WEIGHT FEELING GREAT with *self-hypnosis* and *meditation*

By

Catherine Elizabeth

ISBN: 1-4033-6540-7 (e-book)
ISBN: 1-4033-6541-5 (Paperback)

Library of Congress Control Number: 2002093977

This book is printed on acid free paper.

Printed in the United States of America
Bloomington, IN

1stBooks – rev. 01/15/03

Nantucketselfhelpcenter.com
SelfHelpinstr@aol.com
P.O. box 2893
Nantucket Mass, 02584

DEDICATION

This book is dedicated to all of my students who for twenty-seven years have stood by me and waited for me to get this job done.

It is to Suzanne Higgins who supported my work at Glendale Community College in Arizona.

It is thanks to Jody, Fawn, Merv, and those who stood by me when times were most difficult. It is to Gholdgate, a friend since childhood, and Lita Bowles.

I must mention Mike Boarman, and those who worked with me at Cigna Health Care, without whom, I wouldn't be here today.

It is to those of you out there who are ready to let go of some of the frustration, hurt, pain, and discomfort you've carried around needlessly for so long. Lastly, It is to me as a symbol of my freeing myself up to move on and use the gifts I have been given knowing that As I give, so shall I receive, *That is the promise.*

Losing Weight Feeling Great

TABLE OF CONTENTS

WITHIN THESE PAGES ALSO ARE KEYS TO

YOUR GREATEST POWER
CREATING SELF AWARENESS
REGAINING YOUR PERSONAL POWER
USING YOUR MILLION-DOLLAR REDIRECT BUTTON
SILENT ASSASSINS, CATCH AND ELIMINATE THEM
SUGGESTIBILITY, WHAT YOU SHOULD KNOW
HOW TO STOP IMPULSE EATING
USING THE FOUR "D'S" FOR SUCCESS
DANGEROUS WORDS, AND THE WIANDS', "UP UNTIL
NOW THEORY"
WORKING *SMART,* NOT *HARD* TO ACCOMPLISH YOUR
GOALS.

INTRODUCTION

Did you pick this book up for idle curiosity?
Have you been seeking ways to get off the weight-loss treadmill?
This book provides help.

For over twenty-seven years, I have been teaching students not only how to lose weight with self-hypnosis, and meditation, but how to change develop, or improve any area of their lives using these methods as their vehicles to make change easy and effective.

During the first session of every six- week program that I teach, I ask the students to state three things out loud to the class:

* Their first names
*What brought them to the class?
*And what experience or knowledge they have had about hypnosis or using self-hypnosis in their lives.

Next, I move through the class one by one. As the student responds, I make small comments and then I write their reasons for attending this class on the board.

When the last student has spoken, I point to the list that the entire class had contributed to. Guess what? We are not all that different. We all want similar things out of life.

We want improved health. We want more confidence. We want our lives to be less stressful. Increased self esteem and to be more attractive to the opposite sex often are on the board too.

We want things we don't have, and we want to get rid of things that we do have. Our wish list covers a wide range from feeling sexier to having more energy. We want to fit into smaller clothing, be the same size we used to be and so on.

Many times, my students during the first session will tell me that their reason for attending was that they were "just curious." These students had read the ad in the college paper, or in some public material of a program I was presenting, and something in the ad had piqued their curiosity.

I love hearing that, because I know that as the class evolves, they will become excited and motivated to accomplish their goals.

Learning about this topic is like eating popcorn. The more you learn, the more you want to explore and learn about.

Did you pick up this book because you were curious? Great. Within these pages we will satisfy that curiosity.

Some of my students come to the class because someone close to them wanted support. They didn't want to take the class alone. What is wonderful to watch, is how involved the "drag along person," becomes. After all, we are talking about improving the quality of your life.

Whatever your personal reason for picking up this book, I thank you.

Catherine

EXPECTATIONS AND ATTITUDES

What kind of thoughts were you having when you picked up this book? Were you thinking, "Ho hum another weight loss book"? Maybe you were thinking it was just another scam?

I ask my students to reflect, and pay attention to the type of thoughts they were having when they prepared to enter one of my six-week classes. What did they think about when they prepared to attend the first class? What were their thoughts as they approached the door to the class.?

I do this because it is my lead into discussing how we don't get what we "want" out of life, we get what we "expect".

If you have expectations of just taking one more class, reading one more book, or making one more futile attempt at weight loss, that is exactly what you will experience. However, if you have expectations of success, that is what you will have happen.

Don't worry. As we proceed you will discover how to build the proper expectations into your program in order for you to be successful.

What are your attitudes about planning to really use the material in this program? Are you receptive and open- minded?

Are you ready to receive new information and give it a sincere chance to work?

Could you be thinking of how you have tried so many programs in the past, and none of them worked?

Your mind might be reflecting on your varied attempts of the past and the failure of those attempts working, or having a lasting effect.

If that is the case, you have skepticism and self- doubt before we even begin. Whoa. Stop right here!

Let's give this some thought.

It is important to really become clear on how you feel about this. All things are possible when you believe in yourself, and your ability

1

to accomplish a goal. If there is any appearance of self doubt, now is the time to reverse the thought process that started it. Begin telling yourself over and over how good it feels now that you believe in yourself <u>and</u> your ability to accomplish goals you set for yourself.

No matter what has been going on in the past in your life, or even up to the last few minutes, in your thoughts, if it has been self-defeating or negative, we want to let it go.

Let's focus on today being the first day of the rest of your life. When negative thoughts enter your mind, remind yourself of your desire to let that type of thinking go. We do this with our new way of thinking.

The very nature of our minds is such that we cling to more of the negative than the positive experiences in life. We do one thing wrong, and 99 right, and we will dwell on the one thing we didn't accomplish or succeed at.

We would never treat a best friend this way. Why continue to do it to yourself?

What are your beliefs about yourself? For example, are you thinking that you are not sure you can do this?

Is there a negative belief system of not deserving all of the good that would be the result of success with this program?

This might at first seem like a silly thing for me to say. The truth is when we don't feel good about ourselves, we don't believe that we deserve to be happy or fulfilled.

This belief system is in the unconscious part of our minds. We may think we want something, but it is the underlying thought, the thought in the sub-conscious mind, that will set us up for failure.

This is important to know because it makes it easier for us to become aware of the self-sabotage we do to ourselves. The awareness is half the battle. Once we do become aware, then we can decide whether or not we have had enough mediocrity and disappointment in life.

Get ready to let all of the past limitations that might have been operating in your life leave you now. Prepare to have them disappear like sand going through a sieve. They have been weighting you down.

From this moment on, we will make new positive choices for ourselves. We begin to allow the old worn out negative belief patterns to fall away into the bloated nothingness from whence they came.

What do you believe about your ability to attain and maintain your perfect weight?

What is your perfect weight? Have you given this question much thought? This is time to do this.

It might take some time alone to really develop an awareness of what it is that you *do* expect, and desire out of life.

How has life treated you? Have you been positively reinforced throughout your life, or have you had one challenge after another that you met alone, and felt you didn't do a good job. By alone, I mean with no support systems or others to help you or be with you.

One disappointment after another in your consciousness can create an expectation of failure before we even undertake a program. Seeds get planted in the mind each time we are reminded of or think of our past disappointments or failures through our thoughts. These thoughts (seeds) continue to grow until we uproot them and plant new seeds of faith, confidence and belief in ourselves in their place. It is worth repeating that we do not get what we want out of life, we get what we expect. We change our thoughts, we change our lives.

There is an age-old expression, "what we resist, persists." Translated, it means that if we resist weight and gaining weight, we are getting more of what we don't want.

If we are "afraid" that we cannot lose the weight, we then have very powerful subconscious "Expectations of failure." Fear is a great and most powerful motivational force. We do not get what we want out of life, we get what we expect.

.

In the chapter on finding your motivator, there will be more discussion of fear and what it can do to us. We will be replacing our fear thoughts with confident and positive ones. We cannot hold on to fear and positive faith at the same time.

We will also discuss negative as well as positive motivators.

It isn't so much what we do in life that is so important, as our attitude going into it. A positive attitude won't fix a broken down automobile, but it will give us the clarity of mind, and calmness to make the best choices of how to get it taken care of.

What are your attitudes regarding weight loss or weight gain? Your attitude is the mental position, a mindset or emotion that is inside of you regarding weight. These attitudes have all joined together to create habits. Your habits are acquired modes of behavior that our time with repetition have become nearly or completely involuntary. An example could be that every time you get on the phone, you eat, or something as simple as tapping your fingers or toes.

What are you thinking right now about giving this process a chance to work in your life?

Are you open-minded?

Have you already made up your mind that it cannot possibly work? Start this moment to tell yourself how strong your desire is to become and maintain your perfect weight. Think about developing the positive attitude that this program works. It does, if you work it.

You will see how to apply the proper thoughts to bring about this strong desire while in the relaxed state in a further chapter.

What are your attitudes about yourself, your life, your body, and your work?

Take out a clean sheet of paper and think about these things. Get off by yourself and allow yourself to reflect on them.

Personal notes

Isn't it time you enjoyed happiness? It might surprise you to learn that some of us actually are afraid to be happy. We do all that we can to prevent that from appearing in our lives.

If you discover that you have been feeling less than, or insignificant in this world, that belief system is something you need to let go of. It is a myth.

You are important and valuable or you wouldn't be here. You are an important piece of the tapestry of life.

Within these pages, you will find the ways to let go of no longer wanted or needed expectations of failure and disappointment, and choose in their place, feelings of deserving and being ready to experience total fulfillment in life.

As we progress with this program, we move into an action plan and full explanation of the process, which will take you from where you are to where you want to be.

You will have the formula to not only become your perfect weight, and maintain it, but you will also have the tools to change, develop or improve any area of your life, easily quickly and effortlessly.

When you learn how to use and apply affirmations combined with visualization and relaxation, you will be surprised at how simple it is. You might wonder, as I did, why we weren't taught this in grade school. Why did something this wonderful become so esoteric and hidden from us?

In the special affirmation section in the back of the book you will find affirmations tailored to meet your personal needs or desires.

One of my clients was determined to lose weight. She weighed over 300 pounds. After she saw her physician, we went to work.

The one thing she had wanted to do all her life was to ride a horse. With the weight she was carrying, she was afraid to try. With hypnosis, we used the visualization of her riding her horse, wind blowing her hair, breezes brushing her face, a sense of freedom and joy permeating her entire being, she was in heaven. She got excited and enthused with these images and lost over 100 pounds.

(In meditation we could use same images and feelings)

To contrast, and demonstrate what happens with expectations and attitudes, another client sticks out in my mind.

Her doctor told her to lose weight or else she would die. She came to me for three sessions. It appeared she hadn't listened to anything I said, and she hadn't done any of the "homework" I sent her home with.

This homework consisted of simple exercises I gave her to determine where her beliefs and desires truly were. It was given to her to help her focus.

When she came to me for her next session, I told her I wanted to test her "desire" to accomplish this weight goal. I expressed my concern that she didn't have the desire at a subconscious level of mind to make this happen. I explained how important it was to have that desire present.

You can think you want to lose weight, stop smoking, or change any other behavior at a conscious level of mind, but until it is a burning desire in the inner mind, the subconscious, it won't happen.

I hypnotized her. While she was in the relaxed state of mind, I had her visualize one of those bulbs that you see at fundraisers.

Next, I asked her to see numbers beside the bulb and going up the side to the top. These numbers ranged from one to ten. These numbers represented her level of desire to become her perfect weight. The number 10 was at the top. I asked her to watch the meter as the level of the liquid rose. I told her that this fluid rising was a symbol of her level of desire to achieve her goal. We were using visualization while in the relaxed state, to get answers from the inner mind.

I asked her to let me know when it had finished rising by raising her finger. The higher it went, the stronger her desire to lose unwanted weight.

This, by the way, is how we get direct answers from the subconscious mind. This is called is called using ideo-motor responses.

The subconscious mind controls all of our muscles and bodily functions. When you are in the hyp-noidal stage, the hypnotherapist can access the subconscious mind directly and see what your inner beliefs are through proper questioning.

I waited, and nothing happened. I gave her some suggestions and brought her out of her relaxed state. Then, I asked her what happened? What did she see?

She responded, "nothing." As I questioned her more, I learned that her resistance to making the change was so strong, that rather than see her desire to accomplish this change in her life, she had broken off the bubble at the bottom of the tube and put it in her pocket, so that the liquid couldn't rise and give her increased desire.

We laughed at her strong stance in this case. We discussed her options, and went back to work, from a new angle.

This might be a good time to mention that it is important to work with a physician when embarking on a weight loss program. There can be physical or deeply rooted emotional problems tied to the excess weight you are carrying. Medication can also be a culprit sometimes which can cause weight gain, or weight loss. Speak to your physician.

Now, getting back to the subject, if you do not have the strong desire at a subconscious level of mind, it can be built or created. The techniques for doing so are related later on in the book.

Just for special interest information for you, I will also mention here that we can use a pendulum to access the information within the subconscious mind as well. The pendulum has been around for thousands of years, and it is a fascinating tool for self- discovery.

What you may think you believe at a conscious level of mind often turns out not to be the case. You might truly believe that you deserve success at a conscious level of mind.

You might really believe at a conscious level of mind that you have a strong desire to become the perfect weight but when you use tools like a pendulum, or the questioning process, or any variation of techniques looking for answers while in relaxation you might discover otherwise.

Do not despair. If there is any doubt in your mind, of not feeling that you can succeed, you will learn within these pages how to counterbalance that.

With the use of affirmations, we build the correct attitudes and behaviors to succeed. We explore a variety of methods and ways to allow the old negative restrictive behavior patterns dissolve and new ones take their place.

You will learn how to build a new confidence in yourself. You will learn to develop a new belief in yourself and your ability to accomplish your goals. With the correct formulas we can and do overcome any resistance to change.

Take a few moments, and ask yourself if you can figure out what your real expectations are, and where your desire is to accomplish your perfect weight goal.

My personal expectations with regard to my weight are_____

_____

_____

_____

_____.

Do you believe your desire is merely a wish? Now, remember that this is what you consciously believe. As you use your process, and relax with the cassettes or tapes you cultivate new awareness at the subconscious level. Wishes don't get the job done. We have to turn it into desire.

What I expect from this process is_____

_____

_____

_____

_____

As you were writing, did any ideas just "pop" out of you that you didn't expect? Sometimes that happens as we begin to write. We gain powerful insights and new clarity in thought when we write out our ideas.

Do you expect success?

Do you anticipate "one more" failure or disappointment?

There are specific affirmations in the back of this book. They are written as a guide for you. There are a number of problem areas that we deal with when we are working toward our perfect weight goal.

If, for example, your problem is eating junk and fatty foods, there is an affirmation designed to turn that behavior around.

9

We will be discussing how to choose the most beneficial affirmations for you to use in your program. You might be like I was and choose to use them all.

The choice is yours. Your greatest gift is your power to choose your thoughts.

All things are possible when you believe in yourself. If you suspect that you do not believe in yourself, write out the following in your own handwriting.

"All things are possible when I believe in myself.

I believe in myself and my ability to change, develop, or improve any area of my life easily, quickly, and effortlessly."

Quickly become aware of the next thought that goes through your mind. Could it be that you are thinking, "yeah, Right?"

If so, you simply continue writing.

Sample:

I am now choosing to develop the core belief system of believing in myself.

Tell yourself that you are now building a newfound belief in yourself *and* your ability to change anything develop anything, or improve anything in your life easily, quickly and effortlessly.

Remind yourself that today is the first day of the rest of your life. The past is the past.

You might add things like, "up until now," I haven't been in charge of my own life, but now I am taking control over my life and my emotions. Another one is if its to be, its up to me.

It feels great to know that you are directing your own life. You are empowering yourself!

What is it that "up until now," you have been experiencing in your life, or tolerating, that you are ready to let go of?

Maybe you haven't allowed yourself to make your own decisions or_____?_____, but starting now, you are. Allow yourself to feel that new self empowerment.

Surprisingly, if you get disgusted or angry with yourself, and the way things are going, you can use that anger as a catalyst for your success. Rather than continuing to use anger to sabotage yourself, you can make new choices today.

You can tell yourself that you've had enough mediocrity and tell yourself that you are ready to let go of whatever else has been going on your life that you are ready to let go of.

This might take some time and effort but the payoff is definitely worth it.

You are on your way.

Catherine Elizabeth

Personal notes

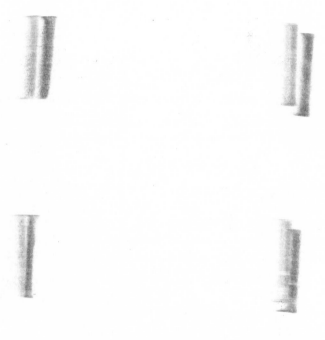

FIRST COMES YOU

We want our relationships to be happy yet; we often do not even know what would make us happy.

We expect others to please us, but we don't even know what it is that we want or expect from them.

The reason for the title, first comes you, is that each one of us needs to know who we are and what we are all about to be happy and fulfilled. The most important relationship then, is the one you have with yourself.

Do you know who you are? Do you know what you are?

Happiness is an inside job.

I remember during my first relaxations where the teacher would tell me to "see myself in a place that was very pleasing to me. He would tell me to see myself happy."

My mind would be a complete blank. No one had ever told me that I could seek out what would please me. I had always been such a good people pleaser. I was always looking out for the other person. I have learned since, that that was my way of not having to deal with my own emotions and feelings. I had frozen emotions.

It took practice to learn simple things about myself such as I am happiest around the ocean. I even learned that it was early in the morning that I loved the most. As I progressed, I learned many other things that were important to me.

Taking the time to do this is not selfish. As a matter of fact it is beneficial for all of those around you, as well as for you. People enjoy being around a happy person.

Your self esteem increases also when you are happy inside. Self esteem is feeling good about yourself from the inside no matter where you are or what you are doing.

There are exercises and more detailed concepts of how you can explore the wonders of you as you read through this book. Never lose sight of the fact that you are an important person. You are special, you are one of a kind, that alone makes you special.

Self-discovery and self-awareness are most important in our lives. Identifying what makes us happy or sad, angry or any other emotion is a major part of our personal development program. We learn about our stressors, for example, and then, by affirming inner calmness and inner contentment, we eliminate our eating as a reaction to those stressors.

We learn to act, and not react to life's little challenges. So you can see how part of the process towards our fulfillment and happiness is to take the time to get to know more about your self.

Ask yourself:

What makes me happy? (Do you know)?
Where and when do I feel enthusiasm?
Joy?

This can be a tricky one. If you have lost touch with who and what you are all about, it could take time to become aware.

A therapist will always ask," What do you do for fun," when they suspect depression. This is often a difficult question to answer at that time. Depression is inward directed anger. Anger can cause us to overeat. Sadness can also cause us to overeat. We are stuffing our emotions. We need to continue to feed anger though in order for it to survive. Have you fed your anger today?

We become angry at another for a multitude of reasons, and we allow that anger to fester. It is futile. In many cases, the other person isn't even aware that we are angry. We are only harming ourselves. The other person is going about their business happy as a clam.

Other questions that might benefit you to explore could be similar to the following.

What is going on in my life that is causing me grief?

Am I holding on to Anger? Am I ready to let it go?

CREATING NEW AWARENESS

Becoming aware of a character defect, and being willing to work on it, is half the battle.

Ask yourself the following questions:

1. Do you feel yourself under pressure to succeed all the time?
2. Do you have a need to generate excitement again and again to keep from becoming bored?
3. Is one area of your life disproportionately important to you?
4. Do you feel a lack of intimacy with the people around you?
5. Are you unable to relax?
6. Are you inflexible once you've taken a stand on something?
7. Do you identify so closely with your activities that if they fall apart, you do too?
8. Are you always worried about preserving your image?
9. Do you take yourself too seriously?
10. Are your goals unclear, shifting back and forth between long-range and immediate?

Think about each question.

If you have a yes answer, ask yourself if this is how you want it to be?

Do you start out being that way? If not, when did you get that way?

Are you in charge of your life, or has life taken charge of you?

Creating awareness of yourself, enables you to get in touch with the real you. You will then have new perspectives. You will have new insight to rethink objectives and reshape behavior patterns. You will differentiate between your true goals and the ones pushed on you by expectations of others.

If you could create a perfect world for yourself, what would your life be like?

My perfect world would be

_____

_____

_____

_____

_____

_____

_____

_____

_____

_____

Ask yourself, "Is it *my* decision to become the perfect weight for me?

Have I decided on *my* reasons for wanting to accomplish this goal?

What is the greatest benefit in your mind that you will receive when you become the perfect weight?

_____

_____

_____

_____

_____

_____

_____

_____

It has to be your choice. We want to create a feeling of enthusiasm within and use that as our catalyst for accomplishment of our goal.

Do you believe you deserve the good that will come to you as a result of this weight loss?

Are you in control of your life and your emotions?

Or, have you given your personal power away to others, so that now you are indecisive and confused when it comes time to make the best choices for you?

Have you been seeking help from others cafeteria style, asking first one and then another and then winding up even more confused?

The true answers are within us. We just have to learn to pay attention and listen to our inner self. We do that when we are in a relaxed state of mind.

Now is the time to begin developing self- assurance and trust in your own inner guidance system.

You can have everything you desire to have provided you are not hurting another person to get it. (This doesn't include the guilt others might want to impose on you when you go after your dreams and goals.)

Sometimes we want to take on this guilt. We feel bad when the only thing we are doing is going after our dreams. When someone wants you to go on a guilt trip, refuse to take the ticket. This type of guilt is not real guilt.

The truth is that sometimes those around us like us better when we are down in the mouth, when we are not feeling good about ourselves.

The zest and gusto of life called enthusiasm comes from going after your goals. When you are enthused and excited about life and living, you are truly alive.

I was thirty-three years old when I learned about self-hypnosis, and the process for using it to change, develop and improve our lives.

The more I learned the more excited I became. I was consumed with the possibilities that exist for us when we direct and utilize our inner power.

It astounded me that in a country such as ours, this simple concept was kept so secretive, so esoteric.

Can you imagine? I lived 33 years before I even had a clue. There is an old expression, that when the student is ready the teacher appears. The teacher can appear in many forms. It can be written material, the spoken word, a picture, a physician.

I have found that to be true. My students have heard some of my message before, they just weren't ready to accept or truly hear it until this moment. By that, I mean they heard the same type material prior to my statement, but, they just weren't ready to accept it. Suddenly, they hear it and they want to make me the hero. No, I am not the hero, it is you. You already know most of this allready at an intuitive level. I am Are you ready to hear?

The process is so simple that I was amazed it wasn't utilized in school at an elementary level.

Every child in our schools should be learning about their own power within, and how to use it. Each child is special and unique. As children, we wouldn't complicate the process.

As adults, we have a tendency to make this process tougher than it is. We just can't believe that it can be so easy. We want to complicate it.

"Keep it simple."

My methods are presented in a straightforward way. Let's not try to make them more difficult, by thinking that it just cannot be this easy and looking for loopholes.

It truly "Is" this easy!

When you take time to reflect on your life, you will see that you have already been using what I teach, but perhaps for the wrong reasons.

This process works. It gives you what you ask for.

What have you been asking for? Where is your focus?

You, today, are a sum total of all of your thought processes, and life experiences. When you begin paying attention more and more to your thoughts, you will see that this is true.

Everything in your life follows thought. Where you live, follows thought. What you wear follows thought. The food you eat is a result of your thoughts. The type of work you do follows thought.

We are constantly choosing our thoughts. We choose to be positive or negative. We choose to be happy or sad. The problem is that many of us have not been aware that we have the option and power to change.

Change your thinking, you change your life.

It only takes 21 days at a conscious level of mind to change a behavior. If you were to lose a limb, it takes the subconscious mind 21 days to realize it is gone. In your mind, you still have the phantom limb.

It takes twenty-one days for an old behavior to dissolve, and a new one to take its place. That is when you *only* use affirmations.

When you use hypnosis, and your affirmation, it can happen immediately. It can happen in seven days. It all depends on how quickly the suggestion is *accepted into mind.* When you listen to one of my tapes, or one you have created yourself, each time you listen, there is a cumulative effect. It has greater impact in the mind with each session. *Repetition is the key.*

Some people go to a doctor, and when they hear they must stop smoking, lose weight, or whatever, they are able to immediately effect a behavior change.

Others are like my client mentioned earlier, and it might take a little doing to effect the change. It was the state of mind when they heard the news. It also has a lot to do with the resistance to the idea, or the acceptance of it. It also has to do with motivation.

We are all different. Some of the behaviors you decide to work on changing, developing or improving, can be successfully accomplished almost immediately and others might take a bit longer.

The important thing is to not become discouraged.

At any moment, you could see the results of your efforts. I remember visiting my stepfather's home in Missouri as a child. They still had an old water pump. When you wanted water, you pumped until it flowed. You never knew what push was going to cause it to flow. That is how this program can work for you.

It is wonderful to have the positive expectancy of a child at Christmas. You just *know* that something wonderful is on its way to you. This is what we want to create in our lives. We want to create an expectancy of good at every turn in our lives in our minds, bodies, and spirit.

For some of us, we cannot remember having those wonderful type thoughts or feelings. We must start today developing a sense of them. We start with small things, and then, graduate on to the bigger ones.

Some of us have frozen emotions from past pain.

A tiny plant on your kitchen can be a reminder that we are living growing things. When it blossoms, we have the opportunity to remember that each of us is precious and one of a kind. That alone, makes us special. As we feed and nurture the plant, we remember that it is important to feed and nurture ourselves as well. Only now, we do it with healthy nutritional foods. We use foods that provide us with life energy and vitality.

It is important to develop an attitude of gratitude. We often forget all of our many blessings in life. Start appreciating your good today. Be grateful for your vision, your mobility, your health, and so on.

When we focus on lack, or what we do not have, we forget all that we do have. When we appreciate and give thanks for what we do have, we get more of it. As you give thanks for your perfect health, the body gets the message. We receive what we focus on. I encourage you to no longer allow those lack thoughts continue. When that type of thought enters your mind, stop it from entering the subconscious mind. Remember the "wiands' up until now theory." Up until now you might have been experiencing lack and limitation, but now you know that you can change that and you are ready to do so. I formally wrote and taught under the name Catherine "Wiands-Annett. I recently dropped both ex husbands' names and instead am using my 1st name and middle name.

More and more you hear about the mind body connection. Doctor's are recognizing how important it is to think positive healthy thoughts.

When you think healthy thoughts, you have more energy and vitality. This concept becomes very exciting.

I know I am going on about this, but I really want to convey the message to you that you do have a lot of power and control over what happens in your life. You are the director. You are the sower. We reap what we sow. What do you want for your next crop?

When I began my own program, I did some exercises to discover more about myself. By doing this, it allowed me to choose what I needed to change, develop and improve in order to have a happy and fulfilling life.

I personally had over 76 things I decided I needed to develop, improve and or change. The first thing was to stop being so negative.

It has been said that over 95% of the people are negative. They just haven't paid much attention to their thoughts.

Tomorrow, all day, pay attention to your thoughts. Pay attention to how you speak about your life, your body, your health, your work, your weight.

By nighttime, you will know what I am talking about.

Thoughts are going through our minds so quickly. We live in a fast-paced hectic society. We often allow all of our thoughts to permeate our being, and we pay so little to the type of thoughts we are entertaining. It is vital to our well being to become a sentry at the portal of our minds. Stop that negative garbage from continuing to cause problems in our lives.

It was my application of self-hypnosis that enabled me to go from a recluse of over a year to a national speaker within 18 months, with an international clientelle. I know, beyond a shadow of a doubt that hypnosis works, when you work it.

I also know that demonstrations through meditation manifest in similar ways. I have had the good fortune to experience that first hand as well.

Through the application of the concepts and ideas within these pages, I actually custom designed a career for myself, and a personal life as well.

You can do the same by using your self hypnosis and meditation. As soon as you allow yourself to "accept in mind," the work is done. It is the acceptance of the idea or concept that can be the only thing between you and your success in any undertaking.

There are some things that need to be present for you to accept your good though. You will not accept if you do not believe you deserve whatever it is that you decide you want to achieve or bring into your life.

What kind of things might be standing between you and your acceptance of your good?

Are you ready to let these old worn out ideas go?

What we see in our minds becomes real in our lives. We want to begin "seeing our good" as if it were already present in our lives.

Are you ready to change any negative thought patterns into positive ones? That is wonderful.

When you take the time to learn more about yourself, when you learn what pleases you and what doesn't, and you take action to fulfill your dreams, remember that everyone around you benefits.

People love to be around happy, cheerful, positive people. Knowing this, you can let go of the idea that it is selfish to take the time to invest in yourself. That idea that it is selfish to go after what you desire holds many of us back.

My book "Self-hypnosis works," goes more into these evaluation processes for a wide range of changes. In this book however, we want to focus on our self-esteem, our self-image and restoring and bringing about the perfect weight for ourselves.

I do want to mention here, that it is important to not tell others about your weight program until you have tested these ideas, and seen them work. Once you have seen some evidence of success, you can then share with the world.

The reason for this is that you might not be completely convinced yourself. Your belief level might be shaky. Once you see results, no matter how small, you have established a belief in yourself, and your ability to make your goal become real. When that happens, you can then share it with the world. The more you share it, the more excited you become.

That very excitement is a catalyst for even more success. That wonderful feeling of life called enthusiasm brings more joy into your whole being. You become filled with enthusiasm. Enthusiasm is contagious. It is a wonderful experience for all concerned.

Sometimes people close to us do not like us to change. They may feel threatened or afraid of the changes you are making.

They might not mean to do it; they might not realize that they are doing it, but they will attempt to sabotage your program. They will suggest ice cream, or bring home fattening foods and offer some of them to you. They may suggest that you go out to eat.

They do subtle things to undermine your program. It is their fear. They feel uneasy. They may think that you will leave, or that some other horrible thing will happen if or when you change

Remember during your process to be loving with those close to you and to reassure them. Let them know that you are doing this for all the right and good reasons. (that is, if you have already told them of your weight loss plan)

Let's explore some ideas.

We cannot hit a target that we cannot see.

We have to have a goal. Our goal is something we can "Picture" in our minds using the "as if" principle. (As if it were already true.)

Now, what weight in numbers do you believe would be the perfect weight for you? Fill in the following blank. If you haven't thought about it before, now is the time to choose your perfect weight in pounds, in numbers.

My perfect weight in pounds for me is:

_____pounds.

We might want to keep in mind here that a goal by the inch is a cinch. We want to make our goal attainable, within reach. We need to reach a little, but we can actually "see' and "feel" the goal accomplished in our minds. Once we reach one goal, we automatically set another, always growing closer to our dreams.

If you are not sure when making your choices, or setting your goals what it is you truly want, pay attention to people you see around you as well as on television that you think look good.

Make a note of the traits and qualities that you see in these positive images of others on the screen and, that you want to experience in your life. As you notice the good qualities, and traits in others, don't forget to reinforce within yourself how good it feels for you to be making these choices for yourself. As you do this, it provides more self empowerment. Begin telling yourself all the new traits and qualities you now possess. You are now using the "as is" principle. We are seeing it "as if it were already so." Fake it until you make it.

Do not tell yourself that you want to be like that person or that person.

Oprah Winfrey has a wonderful smile. She has a multitude of wonderful assets. Rather than saying that you are like her, or anyone else, select the qualities that she or someone else might have, and then, just work on the thought that you are now_____ (developing what skill, trait, quality)?

Now, you get to decide what qualities and traits you desire to demonstrate in your life.

What are they? Do not give up here. It took time to lose sight of these things in your life if you have, but you have the power to allow them to return, or to create them anew.

The world is like a mirror. What we give out we get back in return. If we feel confident, for example, others sense that, and they have confidence in us. If you begin feeling a healthier sense of self-esteem, it is reflected in all areas of your life.

If you want others to be kind to you, first, you must develop the habit of being kind to them. What you put out there into the world comes back to you.

Enjoy the journey that you are taking. After all, this is a wonderful new experience for you. You are building a positive expectation of wonderful things happening in your life. Enjoy the process.

Start getting excited about the new you. You weigh the perfect weight. You are radiant. You are healthy. You are filled with a new vitality. Do you get the idea? Taking charge of your life, your body, your mind, is to be a positive experience. Enjoy the experience. Savor each accomplishment.

Take a little time with the next question. Remember that this benefit has to inspire you and get you excited and enthused at an emotional level.

It helps to speed our program along when we can "feel" our happiness and enthusiasm while in the relaxed state of mind.

When we are in the relaxed state, hypnosis, or meditation, we will image ourselves "as if" each benefit we have chosen had already manifested in our lives. We will see ourselves, as we *desire* to be rather than what we might think we are like today.

What is the most exciting benefit you can think of for becoming "your perfect weight?" Think about it again.

Write it out. Writing out the statement will help you really discover what it is you desire the most. Putting words onto paper makes them have more credibility. It gives your words energy and power. We learn in different ways. Some of us learn when we hear things. Some of us learn better when things are in print. It always helps me when I set my words to paper.

My greatest benefit or most exciting reason to achieve my perfect weight goal is. Here are some ideas to get you started:

Improved health?
More confidence?
Feel sexier or more attractive to the opposite sex or the significant other in your life?
Have more energy?
Self esteem?
Less stress?

Feel more in control of your life and emotions?

Improve relationships?

Fill in your own ideas.

Always remember that this is your program. What is going to make it work for you?

The most exciting benefit I can think of for becoming my perfect weight is:

_____

_____

_____

_____

_____

_____

Let your imagination run wild. There are no limitations in mind. What is it you most desire?

Is there any real reason why you shouldn't have it?

If part of your reason for wanting to lose weight is to please someone else, stop right now. In order for us to enjoy success, we must be making the choice for ourselves.

Reflect on your reasons. Allow yourself to "feel".

Feel it happening, visualize it, make it yours.

Personal notes

Know that we are going to be building our desire on a scale from one to ten, with ten being the highest, to make our goal a reality. We are going to do it for ourselves. By doing this for ourselves, we know that it ultimately benefits all those around us.

Even though we haven't gotten to the section on affirmations yet, if you haven't already done so, please take time to grab a small notebook, or 3x5 card, and write out the following affirmation;

"I believe in myself and my ability to change, develop and improve any area of my life easily, quickly and effortlessly."

You might want to add another part which states that you are now taking control over of your life and your emotions, and now you feel so good about all the changes you are making in your life.

Remind yourself that your greatest gift is in the power to choose for yourself. Specifically choosing your own thoughts.

Place this statement in an area where you can read it often. If others around you are not supportive, or involved with you in your program, put it in a place where you can read it privately, several times a day.

Sign your name to it. Put an explanation mark, or a happy face or any type of symbol to inspire some emotional feeling within as you read. This will give your affirmation clout. It will give your affirmation power. Can you "feel" it? Great!

Repetition is the key here. Each time you read your affirmation it becomes more a part of you. When your affirmations are handwritten rather than typed they have more impact, more power.

What kind of comments do you continually make concerning your weight to yourself and others? I tell myself and others

_____

_____

_____

_____

_____

_____

Remember that when we are affirming something, even in jest, we are perpetuating a behavior and trait. Do any of these statements sound familiar?

27

"Everything I eat turns to fat."

"I just have to look at food, and I gain ten pounds."

"I lose ten pounds and twenty goes back on."

"A moment on the lips, a lifetime on the hips."

What kind of statements do you give yourself about your decision to become the perfect weight?

Do you believe that you are just going through the emotions, but underneath you feel you are just wasting your time?

We need to rid ourselves of that type of thought. Use your affirmations often to remind yourself that anything anyone else has accomplished you also are capable of accomplishing.

Mental pictures make miracles happen. See yourself as you desire to be mentally. See it clearly in you mind the beauty of this concept is that no one knows what you are thinking. You can run free with your thoughts. There is no condemnation from anyone because it is your thought in your own mind.

Take some time and focus on yours life experience.

Do you have negative concepts about yourself?

Where did these negative concepts come from anyway?

Is there any need to keep hanging on to them? Of course not, let them go. It is time to move on.

You have within yourself all that you need to empower yourself and make your dreams and goals a reality. Each one of us needs to free ourselves from believing in external forces, as they limit self-improvement. We want to create our own belief systems. This is the time to decide not to continue to accept what others believe.

Life is largely made up from things that happened to you from the outside world, combined with the way you reacted to these things. We want to stop *reacting* in life and begin *acting*, or taking charge. That is why we are now developing a personal program for ourselves. Self-hypnosis and meditation are *vehicles* that assist us in our personal programming program.

Through these vehicles, our success is inner directed, and goal oriented.

You and you alone decide what it is you really want in your life. You write your own script. You become the author of your life. You become strong in your own beliefs about who can or cannot rewrite your script. You are in charge. You are living your life by direction. Only you can change your life when you are the author and director.

FINDING YOUR MOTIVATOR

It isn't so important what you do in life, as your reason for doing it. When we take the time to discover what motivates us, we are in a better position to create a more effective program for ourselves. There is a vast difference in our motivation when we choose freely for ourselves through that great mind of ours, than when we feel that we have to do something.

When we are moved or called to action by "have to' or even fear, we are motivated not because something would be best or good for us, but because something bad will happen to us if we don't. We might have been called to action by this type of negative motivation in the past, but that needs to be changed in order for us to enjoy success. A negative motivator will bring us negative results.

If you went to your doctor, and your doctor told you that if you didn't lose weight you would die, this is a negative motivator. It can set up a chain reaction within us. For some people, it could actually bring about instant change. Others might go into fear and block the change.

We can go from fear to doubt to worry to indecision to inactivity and lastly to apathy. Apathy kills. Overeating and apathy are emotional forms of suicide.

Can you think of any times that you have been motivated by fear?

What if you have had to face some type of coercion from someone near you, some type of ultimatum that you will experience if you don't lose weight?

Can you think of ways people around you have threatened you? (Lover threatened to leave, spouse growing colder?)

We give our personal power away when we allow someone else to take away our own accountability for our behavior.

It is a personal choice to lose weight or make any personality or behavior change. It *needs* to be our choice and it needs to be for our own personal reasons.

It is part of our taking control of our own lives and regaining our personal power to make these choices for ourselves.

When we make the choices, we alone face the consequences and benefits for our own actions.

Make the decision today to take back the control over your own life and destiny. If you have allowed others to have the control over you, begin today moving towards taking it back for yourself.

I recommend that you say nothing to anyone else. Just take the action and know inside that you are doing so.

If you are in a controlling or abusive relationship, above all keep what you are doing to yourself. This type of relationship does not provide the type of support systems you want or need in a personal development effort. You don't want to rock the boat.

It isn't necessary or even recommended, to tell those who have been in control, what you are doing. Keep it within your own mind until you begin to see some results.

Losing weight is not a spectator sport. You must be an active participant in this work, as in your own personal life. This is your life. Get ready to really live it.

Your greatest power, your greatest asset is your power to choose your own thoughts. I know. I said that before. I might even say it again. It is very important to remember this.

One of the greatest gifts we have been endowed with is the fact that we can only hold on to one thought at a time. We cannot be dualistic. We cannot be negative and positive at the same time.

We are always choosing. We are choosing moment by moment. Remember that it is the tendency of your thoughts today that is creating your world tomorrow.

Are you restrictively motivated?

Do you have to be constantly pushed?

When that is the case, we give up our personal accountability for our decisions. This gives us the opportunity to blame others for our failures. We also will have a lack of personal drive and energy. We begin to push others back psychologically. We will get back at the other person or people, by withholding, procrastination and other negative behaviors.

Can you think of when you might have gotten back at someone by procrastinating?

_____

_____

_____

_____

One cause of procrastination is fear." "Fear- of- success" In our minds, we believe that we cannot fail if we do nothing. The problem is, we cannot succeed either when we do nothing. We stay on the fence always being a "going to-b," or a "going to-do" type person. Have you ever known someone who for years has been "going to?

Oops… was it you??

Can you think of a situation where you did a sloppy job to get back at someone?

How about ways you have gotten even by withholding affection?

Let's talk a little about constructive motivators. When we are motivated by constructive motivation, there is some sort of payoff. There is some payoff value or personal profit in this type of motivation.

When we are looking for ways to lose weight, we must remember that when we take away a behavior, in this case overeating, we must replace that behavior by conscious choice with another behavior.

We take away the eating, and we replace it with say having more energy.

We take away the junk food, and replace it with foods with high nutritive value, and for this, we feel better, we are healthier, we feel energy and a new radiance.

We might look at an incentive reward. This is a motivation by an outside incentive of some type. We are getting something for achieving a certain goal.

In school, it can be a reward for a good report card.

Can you think of when you might have been rewarded or motivated in this way?

Sometimes in life, we want the reward, but we don't want to do the work.

Can you relate to that?

By deciding to become the perfect weight for yourself and doing this with a positive attitude, and desiring and wanting the personal satisfaction and feeling the sense of achievement, then, you have lasting and powerful motivation.

You are not being talked bullied forced or shoved into it.

You decide to make this effort. It is something you desire to do. You build the belief within yourself that it is possible. It is a natural choice. You decide to prove to yourself that you are capable of accomplishing this goal. You become enthusiastic.

That type of enthusiasm is contagious. It will give you impetus to go forward. Now you are getting excited for all the right reasons.

Take a little time to reflect of your life. Break your life down in age groups. What did you do between the ages of 7-15 that you considered successful? How about between the ages of 15-21? And so forth. Write down some things that you have accomplished that you considered successful.

Now, take a little while to decide why they were successful.

Create a page like this:

Age success why

7-15

1. PAPER Route
2. SCOUTS
3. St. ANThony

15-21 Co

1. College completion
2. RAdio Mgt - WVER
3. RA

21-25

1. MARRiage
2. M.S Degree
3. RAdio Job - F.T.

You might need to do what I did. Get a clean sheet of paper. You see, I had the need to attempt to do it with perfection. It isn't possible. We are human beings. My need to attempt to do things with perfection has held me back. Don't let that happen to you.

This isn't as easy as it looks. It took me forever just to fill in a skeletal portion. What will happen though is that as you fill it in, you will discover what the reasons have been throughout your life for doing certain things.

The column with the why becomes most important in your personal development programs. As you look down that why column, you will see a pattern emerge.

Have you been a people pleaser? Are you appreciation motivated? This means that you discover that most of what you have done is life has been done to please others. This can be a setup for your self.

This is like a trap. You do things to please others. They don't notice or pay attention. Now you get to feel bad. You have based your feel good on someone else's responses. What you do has to be done to please you. I am not speaking about being selfish. Just learn to recognize your motivation.

If you do something to please yourself and the other person notices it and mentions it and appears pleased, than that is wonderful. That is a win-win situation. I loved the way this is discussed in that book, "Men are just desert." It says do not expect a man to complete you. Complete yourself, and when you are with your man, he is like desert. So true.

It is about wholeness, and it is about your sense of self. It is about self awareness. This awareness provides the foundation for you to make new decisions for yourself.

Some of you might learn that you did things to win. You have a competition thing going on. You have to be first and so on. This is another trap. As a human being, we cannot always be the winner or first. We need to build some flexibility into our lives.

Find the affirmations in the back which will help you build self appreciation and beginning to like and accept yourself. Choose the affirmations that will help you build a feeling that you deserve the best life has to offer and whatever other one's jump out at you in the back of this book.

By the time we finish the book, you will have an excellent idea of what affirmations you want to use.

WHY HYPNOSIS

Years ago a study of 100 persons wanting to lose weight was conducted. These people were divided into two groups. One group was only using hypnosis, visualization and affirmations. They were visualizing their thighs losing their flab and becoming firm.

The other half of the group used a program, which included diet, exercise, and affirmations.

The group that used the hypnosis, and visualized their new bodies actually lost more weight, and became firmer than the other group.

You consistently hear sports figures tell how they "visualize" their goals. Golfers use it. Basketball, football and baseball players are using hypnosis as well as meditation.

They have learned of the tremendous value and benefits of doing so.

Listen to your figure skaters. Many of them have stated that they watch or "Picture" their success prior to skating. They too, know how powerful a tool hypnosis and meditation can be.

Many of my students in my classes have improved their golf games using the process I teach.

See it. Feel it. Believe it. You receive it!

By the way, it might be called another name. But it is all the same. It is the meditative state of mind where miracles are performed.

Ben Franklin used to take catnaps where he did this type of problem solving. This is not a new process. It has been around for hundreds of years.

Daydreaming is another name for it.

The mind needs to be relaxed for the process to work.

The words hypnosis and self-hypnosis are interchangeable. All hypnosis is self-hypnosis. It is just that when you go somewhere to be hypnotized, someone else is guiding you into the hypnotic (relaxed) state of mind.

It is called hetero-hypnosis when someone else hypnotizes you.

The main reason for offering you my cassettes is that in the beginning of the conditioning process, they are very helpful as an aid. At that point, I do the work while you practice and work with the conditioning process. All you do is kick back and enjoy.

This is an aid while you build your skill in utilizing this peaceful state of mind.

Hypnosis is a powerful tool for self-change and self-improvement. Although hypnosis comes from a Greek word, "hyp-nos", which means, "to sleep," you are not asleep at all. It is not supernatural. There is nothing frightening about it when you understand it.

You are in the state of hypnosis several times a day. Whenever you are daydreaming, meditating, praying, watching television, driving walking, taking a shower are but a few times.

Whenever you are not using your conscious mind to make decisions, you are in hypnosis. You are in a heightened state of awareness.

When you are in hypnosis, you are totally aware and in control of yourself. You might sometimes hear your own heartbeat or breathing while in the state of hypnosis due to the heightened awareness.

Think of your hypnosis sessions as guided daydreams. You might feel day dreamy, or feel light like you are floating.

You might get dry mouthed. Sometimes the saliva glands slow down their production when we are relaxed. This also happens when we sleep, or are engaged in sports, frightened, excited as well as when we are in hypnosis.

If you wear contact lenses, you might choose to remove them when you go through the relaxation exercises. It is distracting to have the contacts moving around in the eyes, and they could scratch the eye. You experience rapid eye movement while in the relaxed state of mind.

Anyone with any degree of concentration can be hypnotized. Some of us have to work on developing that concentration skill. When we use our self- hypnosis, we are narrowing down our field of concentration enabling us to focus on the accomplishment of our goal completely.

We are learning how to use hypnosis to control the way we react to stress. We are learning how to alleviate our counterproductive habits and behaviors. We are learning ways to improve our self-image, confidence and how to handle any situation that comes our way.

Scientists have proven experimentally that the human nervous system cannot tell the difference between a real and an imagined experience. This is what makes hypnosis so beneficial. The inner mind cannot tell the difference between truth or lie, fact or fiction. It acts like a faithful servant. Anything you tell it while you are in a relaxed state is accepted without question into mind.

If you see yourself as overweight, and possessing some negative behaviors consciously, you get to choose what to replace those things with. You enter into the relaxed state and see *the new you*. See yourself weighing the perfect weight, and see the negative behaviors dissolving like sand going through a sieve from your life. You allow limitation to dissolve into the nothingness from which it came.

Today, you are a sum total of your thought patterns throughout your life. You may have one idea of who and what you are all about, and what you desire to accomplish in your life. You might have given it no thought at all at a conscious level.

The subconscious mind is a storehouse of lost dreams and broken promises. It might not have the same image of what you think you are all about.

As we proceed, you will see how differently your affirmations, the things you tell yourself, are accepted in mind between the waking and the hypnotic state.

When you are in the state of hypnosis, you are actually working with the inner mind, which is the part of the mind that takes the images or suggestions you give it without questions.

The mind is divided into two major parts. There is the conscious mind, and the subconscious mind. The conscious mind is the part of the mind where you reason, judge, evaluate and make decisions throughout your life. These decisions are made based on the information received through your five senses, taste, touch, smell, eyesight, and hearing.

The information comes through our mind through the five senses and we form conclusions, which stay with us through life until such time as we may decide to change them.

The subconscious mind has accepted these decisions you have made and has acted on them. This part of the mind cannot reason or judge, evaluate or make decisions. Therein lies the problem. It creates problems because of the incorrect information you have given it over the years.

You didn't always give information to your inner mind by conscious choice. It has been given to the subconscious by mindlessness, lack of awareness and knowledge. Because we live our lives on automatic, much goes into the subconscious without us paying any attention. We are living in a fast-paced hectic society. It is important to take the time to become quiet and still, both in mind as well as in body.

Mindlessness is not paying attention to the thoughts we entertain. We allow negative thoughts to permeate our being.

Lack of awareness and knowledge, relates to the idea that until we know the way the mind works, we don't know what we are feeding the mind and what we are creating for ourselves through our thinking.

We have become a nation of automatons. We allow life to throw us around, and control what happens to us, rather than to realize that we have the power and ability to create what we want to experience in our lives through our thoughts. We have the ability to live our lives by direction, rather than by accident.

Up until today, we might have lived our lives like puppets on a string.

We are now, today, at this very moment, a sum total of all of our thoughts and feelings throughout our lives. Everything that we have accepted into our lives through our thoughts is present in our lives to day.

Much of what we have accepted into our lives is there by ignorance of how the mind works, as I stated earlier.

Would we really choose the negative situations and conditions that are going on in our lives on purpose? Would we stay in the ruts that we get into? (This was written prior to 9/11. it is wonderful to see people becoming more mindful as they go about their everyday lives.)

Examples:

As a child, you decided you wanted to sew. You had watched your mother sew and it looked easy. Your mother threads the needle and then she hands you the needle and some fabric. Within minutes, you have entangled yourself. The material is all bunched up. The thread is all tangled.

When this happened you were a child. With the mind of a child, you reasoned, judged and evaluated and decided, "I can't sew." Now, even as an adult, you hate to pick up thread and a needle for anything. You have already formed the conclusion, "I can't sew."

Let's try another one. You spent a long time cleaning your room to please your parents. When you thought you had done a wonderful job, one of your parents goes by your room, and as they glanced in, they called in to you, "Why don't you clean that pigsty?"

What kind of message do you think you gave to your inner mind here? Can you see how the following type thoughts might have been accepted into mind? "I will never measure up." "I am not good enough." "I can't do anything right."

Another example:

A small child gets up and goes to the table to make cereal. As he or she pours the milk, it is spilt. What might the child hear? What kind of comments might you have heard? Were you told you were clumsy, or stupid? Perhaps the actions of your parents were of anger, and you just gave yourself a myriad of negative thoughts about yourself.

The new term for this is awful-lizing. We get one negative thought, and soon, we are on a roll and thinking of all of our flaws, as we see them.

Throughout our lives, we have received messages from others, and we have given ourselves messages. Have you been one of the fortunate ones who had positive reinforcement, or have you been made ever so aware of all of your defects?

What kind of things have you reinforced in your life?

If you were positively reinforced, you have had a rare experience. Most of us have had the opposite. We not only got the negative messages from those around us, but also because we live in a negative society we hear messages on the television and radio that reinforce

"We are not good enough." We have dandruff, body odor, the frizzes, etc.

The next thing we do, is give ourselves more of the negative. We perpetuate that we are less than.

A negative statement embeds itself within the inner mind. It grows with each additional time it is heard and accepted into mind. We are creating reinforcement of those negative ideas throughout our lives until such time as we say,"hey, wait a minute. No more of that for me."

If there was a seed planted (a thought) of feeling less than, or thoughts of insecurity etc. then with every instance of hearing it again, or being reminded of that thought will reinforce it over and over. So many who attend my classes become aware of how stuck they have been in this fashion.

Many use their childhood as a copout for not accomplishing their goals. Granted, it takes more of a challenge for us, but success does win out.

If we look at the mind like it is a garden, look at that thought of being inadequate as a seed. Every time it has been reinforced, it was like watering and fertilizing that seed. Soon, we have a full- blown belief of that thought that we are inadequate.

That isn't the truth about you though. You are not less than. You are more than. You are more than you might have ever thought you were. You are special, unique and talented. You are one of a kind.

It takes fifteen to eighteen statements to counterbalance every negative thought you have given to yourself, or have accepted from another.

Now, knowing this, we have work to do. If you recognize any ideas you might given to yourself from the examples above, or as you reflect on your life, know that you have the power to reverse the process and do whatever you choose, and do it well.

Hypnosis is a powerful tool to uproot any negative thought system, and to replace it with something you desire to believe about yourself. You get to decide. What do you desire to put in the place of insecurity or any other negative thought system in place within your own mind?

Confidence?

Self-assurance?

Self-esteem?

Perfect health?

Success?

Wealth?

That perfect size body for you?

What is it you want to create for yourself now?

What is your new self-image like?

If you could create a life for yourself, what would it look like? Is it getting clearer than when I asked you before?

Do you like your body, your work, your life? If not, are you willing to take the time to create what you do want?

What would you be free of?

One reason why people gain weight when they quit smoking is that they are not told that every time we take something away, it needs to be replaced with something in its place. It is the same with the eating behavior. We are going to take away the eating. What are we going to replace it with? It is best when we do this by conscious design.

Example:

Now that I am eating less, I have more energy.

You might want to take a little while, and see if you can recall the type of things you have been reinforcing about your weight. Could you have heard something about your weight as a child that is still affecting you?

Have you allowed others to call you names, or infer that you were overweight and you allowed that idea to imbed itself in your subconscious mind?

What kind of messages have you been telling yourself about who and what you are?

Have you been reinforcing that idea for years and years?

What negative messages do you want to change to positive ones?

I realize I have been somewhat repetitive, but it is real important to get how this works.

Here is how the hypnosis works.

We take a good look at ourselves *today.*

We look at our lives the way we are *today.*

We recognize that much of what is going on in our lives today is a result of thoughts planted as a child. They were not *reality* based. **They simply are not true.**

As an adult, we get to make conscious choices to eliminate the negative belief systems that we are now aware of. We get to make new choices of what to put in their place.

Today, for example sake, we have become aware of the fact that we have been holding on to feelings of insecurity, lack of confidence and self esteem. We make a decision to be confident. We want to have healthy self- esteem. We want to feel emotionally secure.

We believe that we are overweight, and we want to weigh the perfect weight for us.

I now weigh the perfect weight for me. I weigh _____ pounds. I feel good about being my perfect weight.

We find the affirmations that correspond with these things in the back of the book. What is the opposite of insecure? Confidence.

Our old thought of not being a confident person is replaced with new thoughts like the following:

"I am becoming more confident with each passing day."

"As I build more confidence within myself, others around me are noticing the positive changes and they are also more confident in me."

Fake it until you make it" is a popular phrase. When you "see" yourself "as if" the changes were already taking place, the work is done.

If you are now aware that you haven't trusted yourself or your judgment in the past,

"I believe in myself and my abilities."

"I now have excellent judgment on all of my affairs. I make decisions easily because I now trust myself."

If you have allowed others to have control over you and you want to get it back;

"I am now in control of my emotions and my life."

"It feels wonderful to be in charge of my own affairs."

You believe that you are overweight.

Your affirmations would begin with:

I am making wonderful choices for me now. I have chosen the perfect weight for me.
"I now weigh the perfect weight for me. I weigh _____ pounds. I feel great. I am now wearing the perfect size clothing. I see myself shopping and wearing the perfect size clothing."

Now you are getting the idea.

There are many more in the back of the book.

Rather than continuing to look at what appears to be in your life now, you begin looking instead to what you want to experience. **Go from where you are to where you want to be by conscious direction.**

Know that you have the power to uproot any seeds of self-doubt, and insecurity and to replace them with new seeds of confidence, and self-empowerment.

You are the gardener. Your mind is the garden. What does your crop look like? Do you like what you have planted?

Well, wouldja look at those weeds?

Do we want to continue to allow them to grow? Of course we don't. Get started with your new crop.

What are all of our choices of what we can now plant in our garden?

Let's make a Ben Franklin balance sheet. List the negative, restrictive habits, and behaviors you can identify in your life. List experiences or situations that are going on in your life that you are ready to be free of on the left side of the sheet of paper.

On the right side of the piece of paper, list what you choose to take their place from this moment on.

Example:

Negative:	**Positive:**
Overweight	Perfect weight
Too much stress	Relaxed and calm
Insecure	Confident
Fear	Faith/confidence
Puppet on string	Taking control over self

We develop the awareness.

What am I all about?

What do I want to accomplish?

We get to choose what we want to experience from now on. We find the affirmations in the back of this book that closely fit into our personal program.

We choose to apply these affirmations to our program.

We write out our own affirmations, in our own handwriting. We read them often. We think about them. They become a part of us.

Repetition is the key. Tap. Tap. Tap. With each repetition, the affirmation takes more hold.

All of a sudden, you do something and you realize that one of your affirmations has taken hold. It is a wonderful experience.

Are you used to listening to others, rather than yourself? If you have listened to others, you might want to use affirmations worded with,

"You are," rather than, "I am" in the beginning.

Example:

You now weigh the perfect weight for you.

You are now in control of your own life, and emotions.

Use this type affirmations until you feel that you are getting enough confidence to change it to the "I am in control of my own life and emotions," and so forth.

We must begin using an affirmation that will build an inner belief in ourselves, and our ability to change, develop and improve any area of our lives easily, quickly, and effortlessly.

We want to find the best way for each of us to apply these affirmations. You get to choose which you are most comfortable with.

When you use your affirmations at a conscious level of mind, that affirmation is accepted. When you go into the relaxed state of mind that we call hypnosis, that affirmation is magnified. It has a much greater success ratio. For one thing, when you are in the relaxed state of mind, there is no negative feedback like you would experience when you give your self that same affirmation in a conscious state of mind.

45

Think about it. You feel fat. You are consciously telling yourself that you are now the perfect weight for yourself.

What do you think your next thought is? You are right. It is something like, "bulpucky." "I know I am overweight."

Right at that moment, the law of dominant effect takes place. The last thought takes over. It has much more feeling than the ones before, and it undermines your efforts.

If however, we are in the relaxed state of mind, we see ourselves as we desire to be. We give ourselves the affirmation as we see ourselves, and it is accepted into mind without feedback or questions.

When we can see it and feel it in our minds and hearts, it becomes real in our lives.

There are three basic steps to everything we do.

1. **We decide.**
2. **We set a goal.**
3. **We get started.**

Most people decide, and set the goal, but that is where they stop. Don't let this happen to you.

Some people decide by not deciding. This is a powerful choice. If that is what you have done, and you become aware of it, then, just take the responsibility for that choice. Know that that too was a conscious choice.

There are many reasons why we sit in limbo. Procrastination is one of them. Procrastination can be a result of fear. Why do anything? We believe we can't succeed. So we go through life being wanna-be's.

If you are sick and tired of being sick and tired, then, make the decision to take action.

Are you ready to experience a wonderful new life, one where you are living your life by design and not by accident? Wonderful! Lets get started.

In the beginning, there might be a slight resistance to the change. We will be discussing that later.

While you are in the relaxed state, what we called the hypnoidal state of mind, we image what we desire to experience. We repeat that image. Repetition is the key. The more often we image life, as we desire to experience it to be, the more we accept it in mind. It becomes more real with each relaxation.

What you can see in your mind and believe in your heart becomes real. The acceptance of the idea is the key. It must be accepted into mind feeling the feeling is important here too, feel it as if it were already so!

The acceptance comes from a relaxed mind.

We use the "As if theory." This means that we see ourselves "as if" the changes we desire to experience had already taken place. Remember, the inner mind cannot tell the difference between truth or lie, fact or fiction. That is what makes hypnosis so powerful.

If we know we are insecure. If we know we have a lack of confidence, and a fear of success, and we affirm at a conscious level of mind, that we are now becoming more confident with each passing day, what do you think will happen?

What do you think your next thought would be?

Yes, your next thought is most likely to be once again "bulpucky." "You know that that is a lie."

There is a law of dominant effect. The mind will accept the last thought we give it. If you are using the conscious mind, remember that it is that part of the mind, which makes decisions and evaluates.

If you tell yourself consciously that you are more confident with each passing day, it is logical for the mind to follow that thought with another. If, in fact, you haven't been more confident with each passing day, the next thought will be a negative one eliminating the positive.

Here is the problem, the last thought is filled with emotion, and it is a negative one. That means that you not only uproot your affirmation, but you multiply the opposite of what you want to experience. You are reinforcing the insecurity, and self-doubt. We live in a negative society. We more readily identify with negativity.

When you go into the relaxed state of mind, that I am calling self-hypnosis, and you give yourself that same thought, "I am becoming more confident in myself each and every day," and you allow the mind to visualize yourself happy, confident, secure, then, the mind will accept that thought without question. By allowing yourself to "feel" that confidence permeating your entire being, you have even greater power attached to that idea.

47

The mind accepts what you give to it while in the relaxed state of mind and acts on it. There are no questions or resistance while in this state of mind

If you are more comfortable calling it meditation, rather than hypnosis, then by all means do so. You must be comfortable with your process.

If you have been insecure and have experienced a lack of confidence and you follow this process, you will replace the insecurity with confidence the easy way. I believe it is a natural way. We were intended to be happy and fulfilled.

Somewhere along the line in life, we lost sight of that concept. Perhaps we never had any idea that we had the choice. Maybe no one ever told you that you were wonderful. Now is the time to get it back, or to decide to allow that belief system to come into your life. It is our right, our privilege, and our obligation to ourselves to be happy and fulfilled.

While you are in the relaxed state of mind, picturing this concept of happiness and fulfillment, it is similar to water dripping into sand. Can you visualize that happening? When the sand becomes moist your idea is sinking into your mind…it is assimilating into mind, it is being accepted.

Another way of seeing it sinking into your mind is to picture a glass of dirty water. If you were to begin dropping clean water into it, it would begin displacing the dirty water. Eventually, the water in the glass would be clear.

That is how your affirmations are accepted into mind. With each reinforcement of the thought, and seeing yourself at your perfect weight, it is mentally being accomplished. It first takes place in your mind, then in your reality feel it.

Each time you visualize your self on a scale and you see the perfect weight in pounds registering on the scale, it is working for you. Each time you imagine yourself, as you truly desire to be, the perfect size, doing something you want to do at that perfect weight, it is working for you.

You are giving the subconscious mind a blueprint from which to work.

First in mind, then, in reality, that is how it happens.

Remember that the mind is working 24 hours a day. What you are feeding it, is becoming your experience. Feed it well. Remember it is working whether you are conscious of it or not. By not being mindful all sorts of things, negative thoughts, are entering your mind.

Soon, when you least expect it, something will happen where you will have an *"aha"* experience. You will do something differently than you might have done it in the past. Now, you have belief in this program. Belief in yourself and your ability is being established. You are on your way.

Example:

I went to a self hypnosis class one night. During the relaxation, I was told that now I choose only nutritional, high energy type foods. I eat only healthy foods.

I hadn't given it any conscious thought. I only weighed 110 at the time.

The next day, I was shopping. The cafeteria had a special advertised. It was one of my favorite meals, pot roast and vegetables. I made the decision that after I did my shopping I would go and get that special.

Well, I had to laugh when I realized that I had ordered a salad instead, and was half way through eating it when I realized that affirmation from the previous night had taken over.

That was what we call" *an aha"* experience.

This is also a good example of how suggestion works. If you are an emotional suggestible, it has a delayed effect. Someone can insult you or put you down at ten in the morning, and it doesn't hit you until maybe that evening.

The reason why I have used confidence and believing in yourself, as illustrations so often, is that I believe we need these components to make our weight program successful.

I would also like to add here that another important component is to generate the feelings and belief that we deserve the good. We deserve to be the perfect weight. We deserve to be happy and fulfilled. These statements must be planted in the inner mind and allowed to become real!

We deserve to experience perfect health, or anything else we create for ourselves by maintaining our perfect weight.

If we don't feel that we deserve it, we will keep sabotaging ourselves. Make it o.k. inside your own mind to be happy. Make it o.k. to take control of your weight and your emotions.

Make it o.k. to be as happy and fulfilled as possible. You are hurting no one when you accept these things for yourself.

Through the power of mind, soon, you will have a song in your heart and be peaceful and calm within.

Hypnosis is often the last thing people will try, and yet it is the most powerful, and effective.

You are already in the state of hypnosis several times a day. If you have allowed your mind to wander, and missed a turn on the highway, you were in hypnosis.

When you are watching television, or a movie, you are in hypnosis. That is why tears can flow down your cheeks even when the story isn't true.

Any time you are not using your conscious mind to reason, judge, evaluate information or make decisions, you are in a hypnoidal state of mind.

When you get into bed, and you feel that lazy relaxed state of mind as you prepare to drift off to sleep, you are in hypnosis. You know what is going on around you like doors slamming and all but you just don't care. You are just allowing yourself to drift off to sleep. (a wonderful time to "see yourself as you desire to be")

We are going to learn to enter that peaceful state of mind by choice, and to use that relaxed state of mind to make changes in our lives.

In the beginning, during the conditioning process it can take a little longer to bring about that relaxed state of mind. Practice makes perfect. I recommend using a tape to help you enter that state.

The subconscious mind doesn't understand why you want to mess up the comfortable habits you have created, so it sets up resistances to change.

Remember here, that the subconscious mind doesn't know whether your habits are beneficial or destructive. It is just that you now have the habits and it doesn't want you to rock the boat.

In the beginning, think of a rock with a rubber band pulling it. At first, in the beginning, there is a resistance to the movement, and then it levels out and moves smoothly.

That is what could happen with you. You might have the tension at first, but it will level out. Once you get to a certain point, it becomes effortless.

Resistance can take place in the beginning as you begin to use your meditation or self-hypnosis. Here is how it will manifest.

As you practice your self-hypnosis, the subconscious mind creates distractions to your relaxation process. It can create an itch for example.

While in the relaxed state if that happens, do not scratch because you are in the heightened state of awareness and soon you will be scratching your entire body you can see how this would interfere with your Relaxation Process.

Simply begin telling yourself that the more you itch, the deeper you go into this wonderful state of mind, and the better you feel. You will be amazed at the power of mind. Remember that it is the subconscious mind, which controls all of your bodily functions; your muscles, your circulation, your digestion etc. it cannot reason, judge or evaluate. Use it to your advantage as you practice your relaxation exercise.

Another distraction could be that thoughts might flood your mind just as you are beginning to relax. This is another way the subconscious mind attempts to disrupt the relaxation process. Just let those thoughts flow and soon they will all be gone and you will enter the peaceful state you are seeking.

Some of my students will cough as a form of resistance. Whatever you catch yourself doing, just allow yourself to be drawn back to a simple awareness of your breathing. Narrow your field of concentration down to what you are doing. Breathe deeply and continue.

Tell yourself that with every breath you take, you double your relaxation.

It isn't necessary to remain in hypnosis twenty minutes each time. Once you become conditioned to this relaxation process you will find all kinds of ways and uses to benefit, quite often in five minutes or less.

There are other times to use your hypnosis than just when you take your twenty- minute periods of time.

Hypnosis can be used when you go for a walk, or run. Any time you are doing anything that is repetitious and conscious thought (making decisions) is not required. You could be doing the dishes, taking a shower, waiting in line at a store. You can be benefiting at any of those times, or you will find countless times for yourself when you can be affirming your good.

You can be imagining yourself, as you desire to be.

You can be reinforcing your affirmations. Just reminding yourself how good it feels now that you get to choose what to experience in your life, and following that thought by one or two of the affirmations you are personally utilizing provides great benefit.

We are ritualistic by nature.

The next time you are washing your hands, tell yourself that your excess weight is leaving you now, just as the water is going down the drain. Tell yourself that the water is carrying with it, all negative energy from your entire being. Let it go.

Take walks. If you aren't used to doing so, take short ones at first. This is not only a stress buster, but has incredible value to your whole being. As you take each step, tell yourself that you are leaving behind any need to overeat, or any other negatives you choose to leave behind.

Tell yourself that you are stepping into the now of your life. As you move forward, with each step you move more into happiness, prosperity and perfect health. Make your program fun.

What type of thoughts are you entertaining when you are drifting off to sleep? This is a wonderful time to reinforce your affirmations. As you drift off to sleep see yourself the perfect size, doing something you desire to do at that perfect weight.

That image can be so powerful. Drift off to sleep giving the inner mind a blueprint from which to work, and the mind works all night towards that end.

Tell yourself also that the next morning as your feet touch the floor, you are prepared for one of the most wonderful days of your life. It is the first day of the rest of your life.

Continue on, telling yourself of your increased desire to maintain your perfect weight. Imagine how good it feels to no longer being a slave to negative eating patterns. You are setting yourself free. You are free to be. Now, see yourself as you truly desire to be.

When you awaken in the morning your thoughts have great power. The first four minutes of the day sets the tone for the entire day. If you are thinking it is another blankety day in paradise, than that is what you will get.

If, as you awaken, you mentally focus on yourself having a wonderful day, eating only healthy natural foods, only eating sitting down, believing in yourself and your ability to make these wonderful changes in your life, and so forth, you are filling your self with positive and wonderful thoughts to get through the day.

This is a terrific time to once again remind yourself how good it feels to be a take-charge person. Get into the habit of telling yourself how good it feels to be in control of your life and your emotions each morning as you awaken. Tell yourself what a wonderful day you are anticipating.

By the way, this is a good time to also reinforce that you are no longer affected by the negative influence of others. Zig Ziglar calls those who are affected by others, Sniops. When we are a sniop we are suggestible to the negative influence of other people.

This is probably a good time for me to mention what I call "silent assassins." They are all around us.

We get all excited about an idea and go to share it with someone, and they sigh, or give you one of those looks, you know the kind... that can be a silent assassin. They could make a comment. Ouch. Silent assassin struck again. Become aware.

It can take the wind right out of our sails.

Now, we are watching our weight. We are feeling good about our progress. We slip, and have something with high calories to eat, and someone goes by and makes the comment, "I thought you were on a diet." This is another silent assassin.

Perhaps they don't even say a word, they just sigh or roll their eyes. This type of behavior also affects us. Much of the time, we are unaware of what is going on.

When we allow ourselves to be affected by others this way, it is like allowing them to chip away at our souls. It is insidious. One look, one gesture, one comment at a time. The effects can be very damaging. It takes only one thought given to ourselves with emotion to have tremendous effects on our spirit.

Weight control is a complex process. We don't need to continue to allow others to influence us and control us and make our challenge even more difficult.

Sometimes the influence of others can be so subtle we don't notice it. My father thought it was cute to call me "Crisco."

I let it slide for a month or two, not paying it any special attention. Then, one day it entered my mind when I was at work. I thought, "Why is he calling me crisco?" After work, I asked him. His response to me was, "Crisco, fat in the can." He laughed.

This is a funny thing to hear, as are many things we hear in the weight arena. Although they are funny to hear, they are also destructive. They make you feel less than, and they need to be eliminated from your life experience. They are silent assassins.

The stories like, I am on a seafood diet. I see food and I eat it. Or, I eat everything I see.

It is exceptionally hurtful when it comes from someone close to you, who you consider an important person in your life.

By not paying attention, you might be overeating to "stuff your feelings of hurt."

This isn't something you might be conscious of. It could be one of those things that have been happening with our mindlessness.

Be aware of comments, jokes, and people's expressions around you that might be having a negative effect on you. It is time to surround yourself with a shield of protection from those hurtful things.

Sample affirmation:

"I am no longer affected by the negative statements of people around me. The harder they try to hurt or upset me, the more difficult it becomes, I just become more and more confident. I am now in control of my own thoughts, feelings and emotions. It feels great to have this control."

NOTES:

When I am drifting off to sleep, I have thoughts of:
From now on, I am creating the perfect me as I drift off to sleep.
When I awaken in the morning, I focus on:

Let's recap.

Hypnosis has power because of the way our minds work. It doesn't know the difference between truth or lies, fact or fiction.

When we use the conscious mind, our affirmations work, but they have much greater impact when we are relaxed.

The subconscious mind is where the habits are formed. If we are not happy with the habits we have created we have the power to change them. We remember that they are changed there as well.

Our greatest gift is our power to choose our thoughts.

Our greatest power is our power to change our thoughts. By changing our thinking, our thought patterns, we change our lives. It is that simple.

Hypnosis and hypnotherapy are effective means of correcting weight problems. During hypnosis sessions, both the psychic and somatic components of the symptoms are addressed. We work on achievement motivation, and assure that it is established.

Guilt feelings and diet rules are eliminated. Correct food selections are made easier.

The client, you, become more goal oriented.

When you use tapes or go to a hpnotherapist, an interpersonal relationship is created. Emotional support is provided.

The subject, you, and the therapist work as a team which makes your program easier and even more effective. Teamwork helps to make things easier and gets the job done.

If you decide to go to a hypnotherapist, please be careful in your choice. Get references. In many states, it isn't even necessary to attend formal education as it is in California people just put out a shingle. I attended four years of training. I finished up with Gil Boyne in Glendale, California.

I am available if you desire a custom tape or assistance. Contact me at selfhelpinstr@aol.com.

HYPNOSIS AND MEDITATION, THE DIFFERENCE

Whether you are using self-hypnosis, yoga, meditation, transcendental meditation, prayer, we are essentially entering the same levels of mind.

We are experiencing altered states of consciousness. Both self-hypnosis and meditation require a relaxed mind.

The main difference between hypnosis and meditation, are that with meditation we rise above our problems and sort of drift and float and allow that sensation of perfect peace to permeate our being. We contemplate.

With hypnosis, we narrow down our field of concentration, and enter the relaxed state of mind to accomplish a specific purpose.

Meditation is the acceptable term for spiritual persons who choose to relax. It all becomes a question of semantics whether we use the word hypnosis or meditation. Both require a quiet mind.

Some of the reasons we meditate:

To effect a change in consciousness

To create an awareness to the beauty, the truth, and the goodness of the soul

To allow the heart and the mind to function in unison (meditation has been called "thinking in the heart")

To transcend problems, or situations, we are involved in.

We meditate to be consciously aware of our thoughts, and to bring our thoughts, feelings, and actions into harmony.

We meditate to increase our level of understanding/awareness of self and life.

We meditate to release troublesome thoughts that have interfered with our happiness and peace of mind.

When we meditate, we "come home." We find. We recover and come back to something of ourselves that we once dimly and unknowingly had, and have lost. Through meditation we become whole again.

We experience that unity with the universe to "become still and know" as it says in the bible.

During meditation we have the experience of God and God's presence. We become one with Infinite Intelligence. We receive answers, guidance, and wisdom.

We all have our personal motivations and reasons for meditating. What are yours?

With your self-hypnosis, we enter the same state of mind, but we do it with a definite purpose. We do it with the intention of accomplishing some specific goal.

With meditation we turn to our higher power, God, and we experience peace.

Meditation is a spiritual word for the same thing as hypnosis. You can also experience the same peaceful feelings with hypnosis, it is just that when we use self-hypnosis we are directing our focus.

In meditation, we allow ourselves to completely relax and then we free float. We empty our mind and just "be." We just remain in that meditative state, most of the time without specific focus, just enjoying the relaxation sensation.

In my school of thought, it is not recommended to just enter that relaxed state of mind willy-nilly.

I do not believe it is a good idea for our minds to just be opened to receive while at the same time, we are not paying attention to what might be entering our thoughts.

When we are entering the hypnotic state of mind, we narrow down our field of concentration, and we control our relaxation experience. We can choose how long we will be in the relaxed state. We choose the level of depth. We have a focus. We have something specific to affirm to bring about some sort of change, by choice.

Using either hypnosis or meditation, while we are working on our perfect weight, we still enter the relaxed state of mind, and connect with that part of us which reinforces us that we are already perfect, whole and complete.

In hypnosis, we give ourselves affirmations, which are specific and relating to specific behavior changes. In meditation, we acknowledge that we are all that there is. We are a part of that spiritual essence that we call God. In meditation, we allow the truth of our being to be revealed to us.

We turn our lives over to the care of God, knowing that as we believe, so do we receive. Here we recognize that all things are possible, when we turn our lives over to God. We know that when we ask, it is done to us, as we believe. Now, we can meditate on the presence of God healing us and bringing about our perfect body and perfect health.

We are using meditation to aid us in becoming the perfect weight.

When you watch a cloud floating by, there is no stress or strain. It just simply floats. It drifts and floats. It hasn't a care in the world. In meditation we can connect with that cloud and as that cloud floats, so do we. We can embellish that thought and know that as that cloud and we float... unwanted pounds just dissolve. Through the healing presence and power of the Infinite being we call God, we are freed of negative behavior patterns such as overeating.

When we meditate, we allow the feelings of peacefulness to permeate our being. We know that the universe is more than we are; yet, we are a part of it. We are expressing life. We are a unique expression of life expressing as who we are. We are whole, perfect and complete.

We allow Universal Intelligence, or if you desire, God, to remove anything unlike his perfection to leave us at this very moment. Just as that cloud floats by, any excess or unwanted pounds are also dissolving into the nothingness from whence it came. We no longer have any need to hold on to it. We let it go.

We allow any reason why we have hung on to the excess weight to be dissolved into the nothingness from which it came also. We no longer have any reason to hold on to that weight. We release it. We let it go.

Here is where the work is done both in hypnosis and meditation. We picture in mind, how wonderful life can be when we allow all negative thoughts and concepts about who and what we are to dissolve, to disappear from our lives.

We lift the limitations that have been placed on our lives through incorrect thinking. We just let it go.

Can you see multi-colored balloons floating away?

As they float away they are taking with them all of the unwanted pounds? Note: Do not use the color red in any meditation. It is action color and we want to relax.

Feel how light you are becoming, as the healing energy and power of god are permeating your being.

Can you see the ocean wave washing up on the shore and then back out to sea taking with it the unwanted pounds? Feel that lightness permeating your entire being, as you allow those unwanted pounds to dissolve and disappear.

Meditate on that for a while.

Here comes another gentle wave. As this wave rolls back out to sea, it takes with it all of your past hurts, resentment, and disappointment.

What will the next wave take away?

What will the next wave bring in to your life? Will it bring abundance? Love? Joy? As the wave rolls up onto the shore carrying with it your desires, touch the wave with your toes, and allow yourself to be one with it. Feel that sense of oneness. As stated before, first in mind, then in reality. First we have to see that which we are seeking. Next, we accept it in mind. Now, it becomes real in our experience.

Universal Intelligence, God, has the power to remove any unwanted experience or situation from our being, but we have to ask.

There is a healing energy flowing through everything. This healing energy is flowing through every cell, every atom, and every fiber of your being.

Speak your word for perfect assimilation, circulation and elimination in your whole being. Speak your word for perfect health.

Feel that healing energy flowing through you right now. Allow it to carry off any weight you no longer want or need, allow it to carry off any reason you might have had for hanging on to that weight. The new you no longer has any need, or desire for excess pounds. The new vibrant, radiant you only desires the good in life.

Keep in mind, the statement that your greatest gift, your greatest power, is the power to choose your thoughts. Feel a tremendous sense of power within as you acknowledge the truth of your being. You are perfect whole and complete. You are more than just a body.

You deserve to experience all the good that life has to offer.

It is your right, your privilege and your obligation to yourself to be happy and fulfilled.

GETTING STARTED, THE PROCESS

Now we are moving on with the premise that you have chosen what you want to change develop and improve in your life.

You also are now realizing your great gift of choice. You are custom designing a new life experience for yourself. This is called living by design.

Oh by the way. Please put your scales away for a month or so. You have chosen your perfect weight in pounds in numbers. While you are planting your new seeds for the perfect weight, you will be visualizing yourself weighing the perfect weight. If you are using your scale during this period of time, it is like digging up the seed before the flower grows. Please put it away for a period long enough for your image of your perfect weight to crystallize.

Write out your affirmations for the specific changes you desire to experience in your life. Write them on three by five index cards. They have wonderful little 3x5 spiral index card booklets in discount stores that are perfect for carrying your affirmations around.

Read these affirmations often. Carry them around with you so that you can read them while you wait in offices, or are held up anywhere. This helps keep you focused.

At least twice a day, follow this relaxation process and enter the relaxed peaceful state of mind I call hypnosis, or meditation.

It is recommended that you have a special place where you can go and practice your self- hypnosis, or meditation. These processes can be interchanged.

Some people believe that it is also beneficial if you get into the habit to practice your relaxation at the same time each day.

I recommend that you practice different things until you find a routine that is effective for you.

Find a place where you least likely will be disturbed.

You might want to take the phone off the hook for this brief time.

You can tell yourself how long you want to be in the relaxed state of mind. I recommend twenty minutes or more for these sessions. This is in the beginning. After you are able to enter the relaxed state of mind more easily, you will find it easy to take five-minute relaxation times. The more you want to accomplish during your relaxation time, the longer you might choose to remain there.

In the beginning, it is suggested that you sit in a chair rather than lie down. This should be a comfortable chair with some neck and head support.

When you are lying down it is too easy to drift to sleep. This isn't a bad thing, but the value of the relaxation process with your affirmations can be lost.

Once you move past a certain level of relaxation, affirmations are no longer accepted in mind. If you want to drift to sleep easily, you can use your four-six-eight exercise just prior to sleep. That way, you drift off to sleep imaging your life as you desire it to be and tell yourself that you are sleeping restfully and peacefully all night.

We are going to use a simple breathing exercise to relax. We will add deepening techniques and a variety of visualizations to enhance the relaxation process.

You are now in a chair. You have just read your affirmations. This gets them fresh in your mind. You tell yourself that you are entering the relaxed state of mind to accomplish your goal. Remind yourself what your goal is here.

Example:

"I am now preparing to enter the state of hypnosis to accomplish my perfect weight goal.

While in the relaxed state, I see myself my perfect size, etc."

If you have several affirmations written out regarding your weight, and confidence, you can work smart, rather than hard by encapsulating all of these affirmations that tie together and during your relaxation process you see the entire picture of all that you have created.

Example: you have chosen your perfect weight. You have an affirmation for confidence. You have decided on what the most exciting benefit would be with you weighing your perfect weight. You have an affirmation for enjoying perfect health and so forth.

Now, you enter the relaxation. While in the relaxed state, you see yourself enjoying that perfect benefit you have chosen, weighing your perfect weight, confident and expressing radiant health.

This process works no matter what goals you desire to accomplish. I realize that this book is about weight loss, but remember that the process works for all things.

As you practice entering the relaxed state of mind, don't try to force it, just let it happen.

Some of us live our lives so uptight that we need to relearn how to recognize that state of relaxation. If you are one of these people, begin paying attention to the relaxation sensation as you are drifting off to sleep.

Become aware of your breathing and tell yourself that with every breath you take you double your relaxation. Truly pay attention to your deep gentle breaths that you are taking. Get back in touch with the life within.

I only recommend that you work on three things per relaxation. Have only three things you want to accomplish unless what you are working on is all interconnected.

Example:

You might combine becoming your perfect weight, the feelings of confidence being your perfect weight, enjoying perfect health by taking control of your weight, being in control over your life and your emotions.

During this relaxation, you might see yourself only eating sitting down, feeling energy, etc.

You can image yourself at the perfect weight, doing something you love to do and so on.

These things are all interconnected and related to your weight loss program. You can combine them all into one relaxation.

You might decide to begin working on career development, or developing some skill, to stop smoking, and to do several other things. Do not do a relaxation with so many aspects in one relaxation.

It will cause your mind to scatter and you will not reap the benefits that you would reap by keeping each session simple.

You have loosened any tight clothing, and prepared your area to relax. Let's get started.

Shift into a comfortable position.

In the beginning, it is recommended that you sit in a chair. The reason for this is, if you are lying down, you might drift off to sleep. There would be no harm done here, other than the lost time for doing your affirmations.

Read your affirmations over just before you relax.

This will allow you to work smart and not hard during your relaxation.

Once again, remind yourself that you are now going to relax for the purpose of_____

_____

_____

I would suggest that when you state your purpose for the relaxation you use words like "to attain my perfect weight goal."

_Now, close your eyes, take a deep breath and hold it to the count of four.

Count *One-two-three-four, slowly*

You might want to practice breathing in through your nose and exhaling slowly through the mouth.

Exhale slowly.

As you relax, allow the tension to begin leaving your body. Feel it leaving the neck, the arms, hands etc.

Now, take a second breath, hold it to the count of six.

Count One-two-three-four-five-six, slowly

At the count of six, exhale, and relax. Notice that you exhale slower than you inhale.

Become aware of your breathing, that gentle rhythmic movement of life moving throughout your entire body.

It is during that period of time when you are exhaling that you can feel your muscles unwinding and relaxing.

Now, take a deep, very deep breath. Hold it to the count of eight, and allow yourself to exhale.

Count One-two-three-four-five-six-seven-eight, slowly

Exhale:

As you exhale, allow the pressures and tensions of the day to leave you. Feel the wonderful sense of release as you let go. You actually feel lighter.

This slow deep rhythmic breathing enables you to "trigger" a relaxation response. This response is the opposite of the fight or flight experience.

Your inhaling should be comfortable and relaxing.

Most of us are shallow breathers. We do not take deep enough breaths. This causes us to hold on to tension, particularly in the neck area.

You will discover that another tremendous benefit of using your self- hypnosis is the freedom from the pain that tension causes, or has caused you in the past.

Experts recommend you work with and take a deep breath at least 30-40 times a day. Take a few before you begin your self-hypnosis session.

As you are relaxing, you may try different techniques for deepening your relaxation. This can include:

You might begin counting down from ten, or twenty to one, telling yourself that with each number that you pass you are relaxing even more.

You might begin moving through your body, beginning at the neck, allowing the muscles to relax. Tell yourself "my neck muscles are relaxing, completely relaxing." "All tension is leaving my neck now." "My shoulders are relaxing, completely relaxing. My upper arms are relaxing, my forearms and hands and fingers are relaxing." "As I allow my fingers to relax, there is a tingling sensation in my hands and fingers. This is a normal indication of a deep relaxation."

"My chest is relaxing." "My chest muscles are relaxing. With every breath that I take I double my relaxation. With every breath that I take I go deeper into the relaxed state of mind, feeling calmer, feeling more peaceful."

This is a good time to tell yourself how you are looking forward to that peaceful experience. You are anticipating that feeling of perfect peace and serenity. You look forward to returning to this peaceful state more and more. This enhances the conditioning process.

"My breathing now is deep gentle and rhythmic, like a sleeper breathes.

It feels wonderful to relax.

I am at peace. My stomach is relaxed. My hips are relaxed. My thighs, all the large muscles in my thighs are relaxed. My calf muscles are relaxed. My feet and toes are relaxed. My feet are comfortable. All of the large muscles in my back are now relaxing. My large muscles are relaxing, like large rubber bands. My scalp muscles are now relaxed. My forehead, my eyes and eyelids are now relaxing. My jaw muscles are relaxed. I feel my teeth separating as I allow my jaw muscles to relax. I am now relaxed from the top of my head to the tips of my toes." "I am calm." I am at peace." "I am relaxed." "I am _____."

You can use these words to make a cassette for yourself. When you listen to your tape, leave a blank spot here to picture your goals, as if they were already yours. This is where you see yourself at your perfect weight.

You might see yourself standing on the scale and the perfect weight showing up in numbers, and you feel so proud and happy.

You might see yourself shopping for clothes off the rack in your perfect size.

You might see yourself participating in an activity as your perfect size.

This is where you visualize and see yourself as you desire to be, not as how you see yourself today.

See and hear others telling you how good you look.

Allow yourself to feel perfect health manifesting in your entire being. Allow yourself to feel a new radiance and vitality.

See yourself on the scale, and the scale registering the perfect weight that you already chose. See the numbers clearly registering.

Allow yourself to feel those wonderful feelings that you get when you have done something, and done it well, to permeate your entire being.

After you have allowed yourself to feel all these wonderful feelings and have reaffirmed your goals, allow yourself to sink a little deeper into the relaxation. Your affirmations are now being assimilated into mind.

Just "be" for a few minutes.

Now, whenever you are ready, you simply tell yourself that you are now ready to awaken. As you prepare to awaken, remind yourself, that you are looking forward to the rest of a wonderful day.

Tell yourself that you feel good about yourself and you feel good about life and living.

Now, whenever you are ready, tell yourself that you are now going to count from one to five and on the count of five you will be wide awake, and feeling wonderful and looking forward to all the wonderful things that life has to offer.

"One, I feel my breathing coming back to normal.

Two; my body is starting to move.

Three, my heartbeat is getting stronger

Four: I feel wonderful, completely refreshed, thoroughly recharged, confident, and relaxed.

Five: My eyes are now opening, and I am feeling wonderful, looking forward to all the good that life has to offer."

During your relaxation, or actually at any time of night or day, you can also remind yourself that everything in your life was first a thought, an idea.

Tell yourself that where you live, follows thought. What you are wearing is a result of thought. The kind of foods you eat, are also a result of your thoughts.

Remind yourself that everything is a result of your thinking. The attitudes, habits, beliefs and behaviors you display are also a result of your thoughts.

If your habits and behaviors are not what you want to experience in your life, you can change them simply by changing your thinking pattern. By changing your thinking and your thought patterns, you change your life. Feel that wonderful sense of personal power when you realize that you are a co-creator of your life. It is that easy.

Your greatest gift, your greatest asset is your power to choose your thoughts. (I told you I might repeat that)

You are right now choosing new habits and behaviors for yourself by conscious choice. You are eliminating negative restrictive behaviors.

You are making new choices. You are excited about the new choices you are making for yourself.

Just think. We are the only creatures in the universe with the power to choose our thoughts.

Whatever you have been creating for yourself without thought, or by mindlessness, that you no longer wish to experience can be changed.

Whatever you might have allowed into your life experience as a child, or somewhere along the life path you have taken that you no longer need, want, or desire, can be changed.

You are now making positive and wonderful changes in your life... See yourself "as if" as if those changes have already been made.

Isn't this exciting?

Today is the first day of the rest of your life. Give yourself permission to enjoy it.

It is the tendency of your thought today that is creating your world from this moment on.

It is ever so important to be aware of the thoughts that you allow into your life.

If you are locked into yesterday, you are not living today.

We ideally want to begin living one day at a time, enjoying our moment- to- moment life experiences.

It is time to let go of all of the restrictive limiting thought patterns that have prevented us from doing just that.

Take another look at what is going on in your world. What kind of thoughts are you holding on to?

Are you holding on to anger? Anger needs to be fed. Are you feeding yours? Anger is a tie that binds. We want to free ourselves of it. Make the decision to let go of both anger and resentment. Tell yourself that you are ready now to let them go.

If you are reinforcing that you have a problem with your weight, you continue to hold on to it. How about changing that concept to one like, "I am so excited about the new personal power and emotional control I have in my life." "It is now easy for me to stay focused on my goals." "I am now maintaining my perfect weight of—_____pounds.

What are you creating for yourself from this moment on?

You now have the opportunity to decide what you want.

When you get a negative thought about life and living, or your weight, catch it, and right there before it gets to go into your subconscious mind, turn it around put a filter there and take charge.

Tell yourself that you no longer have any reason to keep holding yourself back or feeling bad about who you are. Tell yourself that you are ready to live life to the fullest. You are ready to let go of all negative past restricting belief patterns that have been blocking your good. Remember to tell yourself that you deserve it!

Tell yourself what you are ready to experience by conscious choice. Be specific. Write out your desires in total detail. When you do that, you are making choices for living by direction, and no longer by accident.

With respect to our weight, we can use "posthypnotic suggestions" to deal with symptom substitution. Think back of how I ate that salad because of a suggestion the night before.

This could mean no longer desiring junk food or fatty food. From this moment on you now choose healthy foods, foods with high nutritive value.

Tell yourself that any time a thought of junk food or fatty food comes into your mind, you are immediately reminded of your perfect weight, and because that goal is so important to you, you immediately lose any interest in the junk food, or fatty food.

Reinforce that with praise for yourself for the good job you are doing with your program.

"I really feel good about myself, now that I am........." Use your own words. What is it in particular that you have done that is something to be proud of? C'mon, we all can find one little something to be proud of.

We can, through our hypnosis, as well as our meditation, also work with symptom transformation. This is when we change the compulsion to eat, through post hypnotic suggestion, into exercising, work, or some other interest. This is similar to symptom substitution but it transforms our symptoms into less objectionable ones.

Example:

"Whenever I get a craving for junk food or fatty food, I am immediately reminded of my perfect weight, and I use my four "ds", to allow all craving to go away. My desire to maintain my perfect weight is stronger than my desire to eat junk food.

The four "d's" mentioned here are:

Deep breathe
Delay
Do something else
Drink water

Sometimes we just eat for no particular reason, if you set up these four d's as a delay factor, then the impulse to eat goes away.

Another area is symptom amelioration. Here we reduce overeating because we are in control of our eating habits.

Symptom utilization encourages us to accept and to redefine our eating habits. If we have stated for a long time that we cannot stop overeating, this thought is accepted rather than attacked. We then continue to overeat a specific amount, but then that amount becomes less and less.

Tension needs to be reduced because we overeat when we are stressed, and this is where your hypnosis is so beneficial.

With your relaxation exercises, and affirmations, you become a calmer and more relaxed person.

We become more confident, and we allow compulsive eating to be eliminated from our lives.

Experts claim that compulsive behavior comes from low self esteem. By your developing a healthier level of self esteem, it helps the compulsive eating go away as well.

We know that fad diets do not work. They might have a temporary fix. What our objective is' is to change our eating patterns. We want to be free of the negative ones, and develop ones that keep us healthy and allow us to still eat enough to maintain our desired weight.

We need to get involved with our program. Our weight loss is not a spectator sport.

When we are emotionally suggestible, we want to use suggestions, which are emotionally based. In our program we want to "Feel the feelings of happiness, success, peace, etc". When we are relaxed, we use phrases like, "I feel wonderful, calm relaxed, peaceful, just bathing in total relaxation."

Also, when we are an emotional, we use suggestions that relate to lightness, lifting and floating.

"I feel my body becoming lighter and lighter, light as a feather. "The lighter I become, the deeper I go, the better I feel."

"My entire body is Light as a feather." Use suggestions such as, "I feel myself lifting and floating. I am completely relaxed, just bathing in total relaxation."

The lighter you become, the deeper you go, the better you feel.

"With every breath that I take, I double my relaxation."

A physically suggestible person relates better to heaviness. The arm is getting heavy, so heavy, like concrete.

Most physically suggestible people would simply have to use the four six eight exercise, and no deepening techniques. They go so deep so quickly. They are ready to insert their affirmations right at the beginning. A physically suggestible person loses about 25% of the messages on a cassette because they go deeper quicker. They simply lose out on the information.

VISUALIZATION,

We are combining mental imagery, autosuggestion, and relaxation. It is important that we keep our suggestions in the present positive tense, "I have," "I am," and "I do."

We want our mental pictures to become clear. In the beginning, you might not be able to picture things in your mind. This is part of the conditioning process. We need to develop that ability to "see things as if they were real."

As I said earlier in this book, there was a time when all I saw was darkness during my relaxation exercises.

There are exercises to develop the ability to "picture" things in your mind. You will have improved success if you take the time to cultivate that ability in your life.

It is a major misconception that visualization and imagination are the same. Visualization has a variety of degrees. It begins with seeing one object or event, to the stage where one can actually see an object or event in the minds eye.

If you can develop the ability to conceive a visual thought with your eyes closed, just as though the picture was on the inside of your eyelid, you have one of the most powerful tools for "creating" new experiences for yourself.

I would go to the beach, and focus on a palm tree or the ocean. I would look at the tree. I would look at it in total detail. I studied the prawns. I would look, study, and then close my eyes so that I could, "see it in my mind."

I did this also with the ocean, the sand, and the clouds.

There must be a favorite picture in your home that you can practice with. How about a child's smiling face? You can look at your kitchen table, see how it is decorated, study that, close your eyes, and work on that image. Look at the plates, the glasses, the tablecloth, etc. close your eyes, and attempt to see these items in mind.

This doesn't have to be difficult. It does take time though, if you haven't been in control of your life, or if this type process is new to you.

Once you are able to get an image in your mind, this process is fun and so powerful. There are no limitations in mind. We have the opportunity to visualize anything we please.

What we can conceive in mind, what we believe, we receive. First we picture it in mind. If we see it, feel it, believe it, accept it, it is ours.

The ability to visualize has nothing to do with good or bad imagination. Visualization can be created through practice of what is called aftervision.

You take an object. It can be any object. Stare at it for a period of time. Focus the eyes on it. Now, close your eyes and see it on the inner eyelid. See it on a white wall. See the negative of the article.

Practicing this way creates better visualization for you. It is not essential to have this to use your self-hypnosis. It has no correlation with depth of your relaxation. It has nothing to do with physical or emotional suggestibility traits. Some people have conscious visualization. They can actually look at a wall, and see an object.

Visualization is a pattern of individual nature. It comes naturally to some, and others need to develop it. Some of us had it as a child, and shut it off through our life experiences. A teacher might have continually told you to stop daydreaming for example. We could have shut this ability off for a variety of reasons. We can get it back. It is important to get it back.

We all have a self- image. A concept of who we are at a subconscious level of mind. It might not be what you want it to be. You have the power to change it. Your subconscious mind knows what it is today. You have the opportunity to tap into that inner mind of yours, and discover what you are all about.

What have you conceptualized as who you are?

Not happy with that image? What image do you want in it's place? Start to use your relaxation exercises to see yourself as you truly desire to be.

This is a good place to mention that with everyone we communicate with there are 6 personality concepts.

1. Who we are
2. Who we think we are
3. Who the other person thinks we are

It is the same with the other person. Who we think we isn't always the truth, or how the other person sees us and vice-versa.

Lets recap.

There are three steps to everything we do.

1. We decide
2. We set a goal
3. We start

The hypnosis, and or, your meditation, are vehicles, tools to effectively make the changes you desire to experience.

Take the time to get honest with yourself and determine what is going on with your self-image that you no longer want to hold on to.

Decide what you want to experience instead.

Choose the affirmations you believe you would benefit from.

Write your affirmation in your own handwriting.

Use your hypnosis and or meditation exercises to reinforce the new image of you in your mind.

Each time you enter the relaxed state of mind, you provide images of what you desire to be to the subconscious mind. Remember, we need to do this with repetition. It only takes 21 days for an old image to dissolve, and the new one to take its place.

Have fun with the process. Can you see it? Can you see that new person emerging? Isn't he/she wonderful?

When you can see it in your mind, it becomes real in your life. See it, feel it, believe it, and it is yours. Practice. Practice. Practice.

To continue on:

There is an argumentative form of meditation. What we do here is acknowledge the presence of something going on in our lives that we are unhappy about.

We carry that thought through to what we desire to change, develop or improve, recognizing that the appearance of what is there is not the truth for you.

Now, we meditate on what we desire, not what has existed in the past.

Example:

Up until today, I have been overweight, but that is not the truth for me. The truth for me is to weigh my perfect weight. The truth for me is wholeness. The truth for me is perfect health in mind, body and spirit. From this moment on, I am allowing myself to experience that perfect weight.

Up until today, I ate the wrong foods etc. Starting today, I am making wiser choices for myself. I know that I deserve to experience the perfect weight, perfect health

---

We not only need to decide what we want to experience in our lives but we need to possibly let go of anything that stands between our good and us. Are you ready?

Sometimes there is comfort in hanging on to painful negative places and spaces in life it might have been all we have known up to now. It needs to be a conscious decision to let go. The fear of the unknown might appear to be stronger than the discomfort of what we already know we have.

It is all about choice. We see a dollar piece of pie. If we decide we want the pie, we must spend the dollar. We can either have the money or the pie. We cannot make a dualistic choice. We cannot have both.

Ask yourself what is the price I am paying to keep things the way they are now in my life?

What would be the price I would be paying to become the happy prosperous healthy person I am meant to be?

Which do I really want?

AFFIRMATIONS, THE BRIDGE

There is a lot of talk about affirmations, yet so many of my students are not so clear just exactly what they mean, or how to use them. Let's begin with the definition of affirm. *To affirm means to state.*

The big problem with affirmations is that they can be negative as well as positive. They can be silent as well as spoken. Whether you tell yourself that you are stupid or clumsy, for example, or whether someone else does, makes no difference. It is still an affirmation, and if taken inward, it does in fact make you feel more clumsy or foolish.

Always keep in mind that it takes the fifteen to eighteen positive statements to counterbalance each negative one.

Our affirmations are like stepping- stones. They are the bridge that will take you from where you are to where you want to be, easily, quickly and effortlessly.

Seventy percent of the time, thoughts are moving through your mind like gentle breezes first here and then gone.

Most of us do not pay any attention to the thoughts that we are entertaining. We do not pay attention to the tendency of our thoughts today even though they are creating our world from this moment on.

Thought by thought, we are co-creating our world.

What are you creating at this moment?

Begin paying attention today to the thoughts that are passing through your mind. Awareness is the key.

Are your thoughts mostly negative or positive?

Ninety-five percent of us discover that we are negative thinkers. We live in a negative society. We are conditioned toward negativity.

Start today to begin building a positive and optimistic attitude about life and living.

As you discover yourself putting yourself down, catch that thought, and turn it around. Begin telling yourself what I call the Wiands' Theory, "Up until now, I needed to punish or put myself down, and I made myself less than, but that was yesterday."

Now, begin telling yourself that each day is a new and brighter day, and from this moment on you are becoming kinder to yourself.

Tell yourself that you are treating yourself as you would a best friend from this moment on. Would you punish a friend for a mistake they made in life for years, or months as you might be doing to yourself?

I call the negative comments others make to us, "silent assassins". They chip away at our self-esteem. They get to the core of our spirit.

Some negative affirmations:

"I told you so." "What are you wearing that ugly thing for?"

A comment like, "I knew I couldn't do it." Or, "I feel like a failure," is another type affirmation.

"I'll never lose this weight." "Why am I bothering?"

A negative look, a gesture or sigh from someone as you express your ideas, or concerns or whatever to another, can create havoc too, especially when it comes from someone you care a lot about. These actions can be subtle, but they are still deadly.

Positive affirmations"

"I knew you could do it."

"So, it didn't work last time, I know this time it is."

"I deserve the best life has to offer. I deserve to be the perfect weight, and to reap all the benefits of accomplishing that goal."

We accept affirmations from spouses, teachers, parents, peers, strangers, the radio and television.

We give ourselves affirmations silently when we bump into something or do something awkward and tell ourselves how stupid or clumsy we are.

When we feel good we think better because we are in a positive mood. Did you ever give it a thought that when you feel terrific, you never tell others?

When we don't feel so great, we like to tell others, we affirm, how we feel. As we focus on how bad we feel, we actually make ourselves feel worse.

We don't mention it when we overeat, but when we miss a meal, we don't hesitate to tell others. It is interesting that we never mention when we forget to feed our minds.

We can be on the top of the world, and a negative gesture or comment from someone around us can deflate us instantly.

Napoleon Hill in Think and Grow Rich, emphasized how destructive he thought those who criticized were. He went on to say, "Those who criticize ought to be jailed." That is how serious he considered that negative influence to be.

When you give some thought to how many affirmations it takes to turn around every negative one you have given to yourself, or allowed someone else to give to you, you then can see how damaging the negative thoughts are.

What is important today, and from this moment on, is to become so aware of our thoughts and pay close attention to what we are allowing to enter our subconscious mind. We need to also become aware of what others close to us are saying and how it affects us.

Years ago, I was driving on the freeway and I came upon a billboard with a picture of a girl who reminded me of my deceased sister. Although she had died over thirty years ago, my mood went from one of calmness and happiness to depression, and I caught myself thinking of all the reasons to feel bad because she died so young etc.

It happens in an instant. We think thoughts faster than we read or speak. Seventy percent of the time, thoughts are flying through our minds. What is going through your mind? Begin paying close attention.

One of the exercises I enjoy doing in my classes is that I set a timer for five minutes. Then, I just stay silent, and allow my students to become aware of the thoughts they are experiencing. Many times they are amazed at the amount of thoughts, and the range of topics that go through their minds.

You might want to give that a try. You will be surprised I am sure.

Writing is an excellent way to become aware of what is going on inside of you. As you write, things come to the surface that might surprise you. You will gain new clarity of thought. It becomes a wonderful tool in this program. This is called keeping a journal. I highly recommend it.

Your greatest asset as a human being is the power to choose your own thoughts. Take dominion over your life by breaking the negative thought patterns and replacing them with positive ones.

Lets' say you really messed up. You are now thinking about it. Your mind focuses on it. You wind up with a thought similar to "I've made a fool of myself." "Why do I do this over and over?"

Most of the time, this is where we would leave a thought like that one. From this moment on, as you become more mindful of your thoughts, you will get to push the "million dollar redirect button", (another Wiands' concept)

We need to break the cycle. We get the same old results because we keep doing things the same way.

Begin to tell yourself, "O.k. I messed up." "This is the last time this is going to happen." "I am chalking this up to experience and using it as an opportunity to learn, but from this moment on, I am letting go of this behavior."

We all have our own terminology. As you read these comments here, modify them to include your own words.

The important thing is learning what thoughts keep coming back. What kind of thought patterns flow through your mind over and over?

These are the ones you want to catch, so that you can write an affirmation to counterbalance each thought pattern that you want to eliminate. You are now preparing to develop a new behavior pattern.

If you are a positive person, it is important to know that there are people out there who will be drawn to you and zap your energy. In the business we call them psychic vampires.

Have your ever felt like a million bucks, and a certain person will come over and visit you, and when that person is gone, suddenly you are exhausted?

Did that person get to dump all of their problems, and challenges on you and then go away uplifted, while you are left in the pits? I have heard this referred to as psychic vampirism.

The problem with this situation is that if you are an emotional suggestible, you are not connecting the incident of this person visiting you and your reaction to it later.

Part of our becoming aware of what is going on in our lives is the awareness of the people around us, and how we are interacting with them. Do you think that after that negative person left and you felt zapped that you might nibble? Of course!

That is a reaction. By becoming more mindful, we catch the situation as it is taking place and we take some form of action. We then are also aware of the temptation to grab some food that we really do not want or need.

In the twelve step programs, the word h-a-l-t is often referred to. It is a reminder word telling us that when we are hungry, angry, lonely or tired, our resistance is down. These are times when we are vulnerable to fall into our bad habits.

When we are angry, we eat. When we are lonely, we eat. When we are tired, we are more likely to eat without paying attention. We eat, and we don't pay attention to how much we eat. Can you think of times when this has applied to you?

Now, getting back to our affirmations, I want to share a few more things. There are some requirements to meet in order for your affirmation program to be successful.

We need to have the *desire-*

Truly desire to make changes or develop new skills and abilities. If it doesn't appear to be present in your life, use an affirmation to make it be.

Example*; my desire to become the perfect weight is a ten on a scale from one to ten. I have such a strong desire to maintain my perfect weight, that whenever any urge to eat junk or fatty food comes to mind, I am immediately reminded of my perfect weight. The urge to eat goes away.*

We need the *information- knowledge*

You need correct information on how to accomplish your goals, how to set your goals, and how to use affirmations to guide you to the realization of your goals.

We need *repetition-*

You must repeat your affirmations often to yourself. Read them often. Let them become a part of you. Think about them, Feel them, and internalize them.

While working on a behavior pattern change, never ever put a time limit on yourself. It will create unneeded tension. Never give yourself a date for say weighing a certain weight. Give yourself a break. The program will work. You do not need any self made constraints or roadblocks to contend with.

USING AFFIMATIONS EFFECTIVELY

A. Consciously decide what, if anything, you want to change develop or improve in your life. This book is focused on attaining your weight goal, so we will put that here. Some of you don't want to change anything and that is o.k. As long as you remember that that too is a choice.

Decide at this point what special skills you would like to develop. Be reasonable. If you have never swam, set a reasonable limit on what you can do in the beginning and when you accomplish that, you set another goal. Don't try to swim the entire pool length five times the first attempt.

Your affirmations for accomplishing this type of goal would include such things as developing coordination, stamina, etc.

For your weight goal, you decide what your perfect weight would be, in pounds.

You write it out in numbers. You become very specific.

B. Set your goal. Write out your affirmations for the accomplishment of that goal. Ask yourself what attributes, attitudes, behaviors do you need to accomplish this goal. List them. Write the corresponding affirmations to use.

What personal behaviors do you need to let go of? List them. Write out an affirmation that you are free of _____ whatever you have determined you need to be free of.

What habits do you need to develop?

Write your affirmations that you already possess these habits.

C. Get started.

Are you procrastinating?

Do not use the word procrastination in your affirmation. Use something like I have a do-it-now attitude and I do things as they need to be done.

List whatever you might be doing to hold yourself back. Write an affirmation that you are no longer___doing_____whatever you have discovered you were doing to hold yourself back.

If you are not certain of what you are doing to limit yourself, and hold yourself back, then, work smart rather than hard, and affirm that you are letting go of *any* need to hold yourself back, or to limit yourself. Allow your subconscious mind to do its work.

Your goal is your objective.

Your affirmations are the stepping-stones to get you there. This is why I call affirmations the bridge.

Affirmations will carry you from one point to the other. THEY WILL TAKE YOU FROM WHERE YOU ARE TO WHERE YOU WANT TO BE.

Using your meditation and self-hypnosis, they will take you quickly… as if by magic.

Let's relate this to your weight program. You have decided to become the perfect weight for you. You have chosen the perfect weight in mind and in numbers.

Next, you take a look at your eating behaviors in order to eliminate the problematic ones.

Choose the affirmations in the back of the book that match up with your personal life.

Are you a junk food junkie? In that case you would choose the affirmation that you no longer crave junk food or fatty foods, etc.

Write the affirmations that you select to use out on three by five cards or in a small notebook that you can carry around and read often. They have wonderful spiral flip cards now in most drugstores or places like kmart or walmart the size of a 3x5 card. They are easy to write in, and easy to carry around. I highly recommend you purchase one and begin using it today.

What are doing now is giving your subconscious mind a blueprint, a set of plans, a guide.

Part of your plan is to use your four-six-eight self-hypnosis technique. You might choose the meditation concepts at this time.

At least twice a day, you will take time to relax, and while in the relaxed state, using the "as if" principle see yourself as you truly desire to be, doing whatever it is you desire to do.

You allow yourself to get the feelings that you get when you have done something well. Remember, if you cannot remember having that feeling, it can be acquired.

Start small. Do one thing you feel good about consciously. This can be simple, and it can be something you do anonymously. I have a friend who puts coupons on products in the store for others to use. It doesn't have to be a huge thing.

You have done something you can feel good about.

Become aware of the sensation of feeling good. Allow yourself to totally experience those feelings.

Now, when you visualize, feel those good feelings again, and repeat to yourself when you use your relaxation how wonderful it is to feel good about yourself.

When you write your affirmations out, remember to handwrite rather than type. The subconscious mind accepts it more quickly when it is in your own handwriting. You have personalized it.

I suggest only one affirmation per card. I used to put happy faces or things that made me smile at the end to give them life.

Every time you read or think about your affirmations, they become more real. They become a part of you. You will soon catch yourself thinking about them even when you are not reading them.

This is wonderful. It means you have accepted the idea and are now embodying it. All of a sudden, you just know that whatever you have been affirming is yours. It is exciting.

Example: One of my affirmations mentions that you never eat standing up. It states that you always sit down to eat. It goes on to say that a small portion of food completely satisfies your appetite.

Many of us nibble while we cook. We do not realize how much we are eating. When the body is in the standing position, we do not get that full signal from the brain. We can eat more and not feel like we have eaten anything at all.

Now, suppose you are using that affirmation that you only eat sitting down. You have been repeating that affirmation to yourself and reading it. Now, you get *an aha* because one day, when you are cooking your affirmation comes to mind, and you stop eating while you are standing up. It is exciting when that happens.

It is a subtle thing. Quite often, you do not realize what you have done until later on. This makes you feel good. You know your program is working.

When you are writing your affirmations, always keep them in the present positive tense.

"I have." "I am." "I do"

Never use progressives, "I am going to."

The subconscious mind is very literal and takes everything you give to it just as you give it. If you tell the mind that you are going to, it will keep what you desire in the future rather then bring it to the present."

Never use "try," "trying to" "able to," or "can."

We all *can.* To say you can, or you are able to do something, means nothing.

When you say you are *trying* to, that implies to the inner mind that you cannot, otherwise you would be doing, not *trying* to.

You will become aware of how many people say, "I am trying to lose weight." Now, you have a little secret. You can see why they keep trying, rather than accomplish their goal.

Never use comparatives.

Don't compare yourself to others. We don't always know what is going on in someone else's life. They may appear altogether on the outside, but you do not know what is going on in their lives.

To say "I am doing better than…" can be dangerous, because we don't really know how that person is doing.

Be strictly personal, when you write your affirmations use, "I, me, my."

This is your program. It is about you.

Be absolutely positive. Avoid the words, "not," or "don't."

If you are writing an affirmation to eliminate procrastination, it is best not to use the word procrastinate. Change procrastination into the opposite, and write instead something like, "I have a do-it-now attitude and I do things as they need to be done." Now, you can embellish that by adding words like easily, quickly, and effortlessly.

Never put a time limit on a behavior change.

When you do this, it will only create stressors, and that will undermine your efforts. The closer the date that you have set gets, the more tension will be created. You could be so close to realizing your goals, and because of the pressure created by having a time limit, you become stressed and begin bingeing.

Keep in mind that you are a unique individual. Allow yourself to open up like a flower in order for the entire world to see your beauty.

Some of you might see overnight results, others might take a little longer for benefits to start showing. We are all different. It depends on variables, which cannot be measured. How deep is that belief system that you can't accomplish something?

How strong is your *motivation?*

What is your *level of desire* to accomplish the change?

You get the idea?

Don't try to *force the change*.

Allow yourself to unfold. We don't look at a flower and say, "open up." We allow nature to do its work.

Be patient with yourself.

We didn't get the way we are in one day. No, I am not trying to be negative. I just want to remind you that we are human beings. Treat yourself kindly and have patience.

If you go to the doctor, and get a prescription with the recommendation to take it until it is gone, it is a temptation to stop taking it as soon as we think we feel better. That opens the door for the illness to return. It is the same with your affirmations.

You might begin noting good changes taking place and stop using your affirmations before the new behaviors are completely established, or the old ones completely dissolved. Be certain that your new habits are definitely established.

To be effective with the program, we need to change old behaviors, and thought patterns. It becomes a new way for many of us to live. I guarantee you though, the benefits that you will reap, make it worth it.

The only way to permanent weight loss is nutrition education, and new habits and behaviors relating to our eating pattern. Lets make this program work by doing it right.

If we were pumping for water, we don't know when the last push on the pump would bring the gush of water. That is how it is with our affirmations. We can be so close and yet it is a temptation to give up. We become discouraged. Don't do that. Have patience.

Once you get your weight under control, you might discover that you are falling back into the old habits of overeating or eating the wrong foods, etc. If you find that happening in your life, you just get right back on track with your self- hypnosis and or your meditation.

Hopefully, once you see how powerful this combination of relaxation, autosuggestion, and visualization is, you will continue to use it.

I use it everyday. If I see someone handicapped, I thank God for my perfect health. When I look at a beautiful flower or tree, I thank God for Life, and the beauty in my life.

If you are not a God Person, perhaps you can do what I did when I first started. I thanked Infinite Intelligence. Let's face it, something is happening in this universe. There is life everywhere. We are not all at the same McDonald's at the same time. We don't make the world tip over because everyone is in the same place. There is a presence or essence in this universe that is continually operating.

I even have to laugh at myself sometimes. This powerful vehicle for change is so easy to use, and I know beyond a shadow of a doubt that it works! and yet, even I from time to time will begin to slip back into some of my old ways.

We live in an instant society. Everything has to be instant. We shift our attentions and we continually change and evolve. It doesn't take too long if we are not paying attention for a long-standing negative behavior to return, but if you catch it and deal with it right when you become aware of it, you remain in control.

Don't get discouraged.

You can be so close to the accomplishment of your goal and get discouraged. Don't do this. Hang in there. This stuff works.

How many affirmations can you use?

You can use as many affirmations as you desire to use. I had affirmations to change, develop improve over 76 aspects of my life. I had a stack of index cards that I read continuously.

I carried them in a number 10 envelope on 3x5 cards. I can't tell you how many envelopes I wore out. Now, they have wonderful spiral index card booklet type things at most of your discount drugstores.

However, as I mentioned before, when you use your relaxations, your self-hypnosis or meditation, to make the changes in your life, you want to use no more than three affirmations per relaxation, unless the affirmations you are using are all interconnected.

For example, you have decided to become the perfect weight for you. You have chosen the weight in numbers. You have become aware of your greatest motivation for wanting to accomplish this goal. All of the benefits of becoming this perfect weight such as perfect health, being attractive to the opposite sex, feeling good about yourself, self-esteem, and so on can be merged into your images as you are in the relaxed state of mind and "seeing yourself as if these changes had already taken place."

You are in the relaxed state and affirming these things, and you see yourself in a store maybe picking out a certain size clothing off the rack.

You are still in the relaxed state and you feel yourself smiling and feeling so happy.

It is pleasurable. It is healthy. It is beneficial. And it gets results. Self-hypnosis and meditation work!

WARNING

AFFIRMATIONS CAN BE DANGEROUS!

HOW? There is a danger when you believe that if you write out your affirmations and read them often, that everything is all right, and voila the work is done. Not so.

You do need to take some type of action along with reading and thinking of and internalizing your affirmations. The relaxation, is the most important part. Taking the time to relax and internalize your affirmations pays big benefits. This is participating in your weight program.

You cannot program yourself for success, instant wealth, becoming the perfect weight without taking some other types of action to make it happen.

You will have a degree of success just by using the affirmations, but to enjoy true success remember, "If it's to be it's up to me."

Don't wait for someone to wave a magic wand for you.

When you have knowledge,that is terrific. There are slogans, which read that knowledge is power. That is not the truth though. It is *applied* knowledge that is the power.

The most effective way to use your affirmations is to go into the relaxed state of mind. When you are relaxed physically, the mind also relaxes and the information you are giving it goes directly to the power under the hood. While relaxed, your affirmations and images are accepted right where behaviors and habits are established. With practice and with repetition, the old behavior dissolves, and the new one takes its place. Tap. Tap. Tap.

Have you ever seen a rock that has had water dripping on it, or rocks at the ocean that have been worn by the constant flow of water? The water dripping or flowing through the rocks over a period of time have caused marks or dents in the rocks. With repetition, your affirmations are making changes in your thoughts and in how you perceive yourself at a subconscious level of mind.

We are eliminating the negative concepts, which had no reality basis for being there in the first place, and replacing them with the truth for you.

That truth is that you are whole perfect and complete just as you are. You are a unique and precious human being. It is your right, privilege and obligation to yourself to be happy and fulfilled.

Many of us did not get that type of message as we were growing up. Now as adults, we are going to re-parent ourselves via affirmations. We are going to make it o.k. To be who we are. We are going to accept ourselves unconditionally as our own best friend. We are recognizing that we deserve to be happy.

This is the time to virtually create a new world for you. Get rid of the garbage type thinking. Let go of all of the restrictive and limiting behaviors that have been created in your life, for whatever reason.

Be kind to yourself. As they say, Rome wasn't built in a day. It took time for us to create our world as we see it today, and it might take some time to re-create it.

Introspection is like peeling an onion. We do this a layer at a time. As we are ready for new insight and understanding, it comes. It comes in a natural and wonderful way. I believe this happens through our higher power, God.

The only ingredient necessary is a willingness to accept the knowledge and to make the changes by choice that will improve the quality of our lives.

God only gives us what we ask for, what we are truly seeking. We need to let what we desire be known. We do this in the silence. We do this in the meditative state. We do this privately. It is that connection that brings forth what we seek.

We are working with a conditioning process. It may be easy for you to enter the relaxed state of mind, or it might take some time for you to get used to it, as it did me. Don't try. Let it happen.

Remember, we live in a fast-paced hectic society these days. Everything is instant. We have instant news worldwide. We have high technology all around us. The world is appearing to be on some sort of accelerated path.

Each one of us has to choose to stop off for a while. We need to take time to "be still and know."

There is a part of us that already knows that intuitively. We just might have never allowed ourselves to "listen." When you do, it is a wonderful experience.

What is it you think you want out of life?

What is it you really want?

What are you willing to do to get it?

The best investment you can make in this life is an investment in yourself. That is one investment that can never be taken away. It won't be lost.

Affirmations work. I know. It was the use of affirmations that enabled me to go from a recluse of over a year, to a national speaker with an international clientele in 18 months.

All things are possible when you believe in yourself.

If there is any way I can assist you in your personal Development Program, contact me at helpinstr@aol.com. I offer custom tapes, keynote speeches, seminars workshops also.

AFFIRMATIONS FOR CHANGING EATING PATTERN AND ATTAINING YOUR PERFECT WEIGHT GOALS.

I weigh _____ pounds. (Choose the weight you desire to be in pounds and write it out in numbers)

I take time every day to use my 4-6-8-relaxation exercise to reinforce my personal goals and affirmations.

I look great. I feel great. Now that I am eating less, I have more energy.

I no longer crave junk food or fatty foods.

I am more selective of the foods I eat now.

I am a 10 on the scale of desire which ranges from one to ten in my desire to maintain my perfect weight.

The benefits and rewards of being healthier, thinner and more slender are more important to me now than eating foods that I know are wrong for me.

I am no longer affected by the conditions that in the past would have caused me to eat or drink the wrong foods. They are in the past and cannot affect me now in any way.

The suggestions I am now giving myself are beginning to affect me at this very moment, and they carry over into my everyday life.

I am already feeling the pounds melting away. The inches are disappearing, as I visualize myself becoming slimmer, healthier and more confident.

I see myself at my perfect weight shopping for my wardrobe in the perfect size. It is exciting.

In the past, I identified with eating the wrong foods and being heavy. I am now changing my patterns of thinking and eating. I identify with being thinner and healthier.

Each time I am tempted to eat or drink any foods that are wrong for me, I say no, to myself, and I mean it. My desire to be the perfect weight for me is so strong that when I go to eat the wrong foods, immediately I am reminded of the perfect weight for me in pounds, and the urge to eat junk or fatty food goes away.

More each day, I lose desire for foods high in carbohydrates and choose instead foods that are high in protein. I find myself eating less and enjoying it more.

I choose foods with high nutritive value.

I choose foods that provide me with energy.

I never eat standing up. I always sit down. I chew my foods well. I eat slowly, and a small portion of food completely satisfies my appetite.

Whenever an urge to eat junk food or fatty foods enters my mind, I am immediately reminded of my strong desire to be the perfect weight for me. The number of pounds I desire to weigh comes into my mind, and because my desire is so strong to be the perfect weight for me, the urge to eat the junk food goes away.

Whenever I think of eating junk or fatty foods, or eating compulsively, I remember the four d's.

I deep breathe,

I drink water,

I delay,

I do something else, and the impulse to eat goes away.

I meditate on the wonders of me. Just think, there is only one of me in the entire universe. I am special. I am unique. I am precious.

I know that there is a higher power that provides me with the strength and the motivation to accomplish my goals.

In my meditation I connect with that Universal Power. I am renewed. I allow the healing presence of that higher power to remove anything unlike the perfection that I truly am from my life.

I no longer have any reason to punish myself by overeating.

I am now accepting myself as my own best friend. I am treating myself as I would a best friend.

I respect and like the real me more every day. As I learn to take better care of myself, it is reflected in my image. It is reflected in my walk, and in all areas of my life. I am becoming my own best friend.

Other people are seeing those marvelous changes in me.

I am radiant. I am filled with a new enthusiasm about life and living.

I feel wonderful. I am wonderful.

I am becoming more calm and more relaxed with each passing day. I am calm and relaxed in any and all situations.

My life is becoming more and more peaceful within.

I am letting go of the past, and I am learning to live in the here and now. I see only good all around me. I know that I am a part of all the good I see. I like being me.

I am letting go of all past hurts and disappointments. I am closing the door gently on the past, and opening new channels to the future. I am filled with expectation of good and more good, enough to share and enough to spare. My good can never be denied.

As I forgive others who might have appeared to have harmed me in any way as well as myself, wonderful things are happening in my life.

I am letting all resentment dissolve into the nothingness from which it came. I am replacing any feelings of anger and resentment with warm and loving thoughts about life and living.

Because I now realize how anger and resentment affects the body, and because I have chosen to treat myself good, I now release any thoughts which are negative and hurtful, not only to others, but to myself.

I am also free from judgment and criticism of others and myself. Because I respect and appreciate the differences in others, I also respect and appreciate the differences in myself. These differences are what make me unique and special.

I focus on myself. I am so busy improving the quality of my own life; I no longer have the time or desire to be focusing on others. I no longer have the time or desire to criticize or judge others.

My good comes in many forms, perfect weight, excellent health, serenity and abundance.

I am now also releasing any thoughts of greed, or envy. I recognize that there is enough to share and enough to spare in this universe. I also acknowledge that whatever anyone else has ever done, I am also capable of doing. Whatever others possess, I am also capable of bringing into my life through the power of my mind.

I use affirmations, relaxation and visualization to bring those things, which I desire into my life.

I know that my good is as close to me as my hands and feet. I feel the presence of my good. I am filled with expectation of my good.

What I focus on becomes mine. All that I have to do is accept it. I accept and claim my good now.

My good comes in so many forms. The mind is unlimited. I only need to become aware of that which I desire. I accept it into my life.

I give thanks for what I have now and I am giving thanks every day for my many blessings. I know that the more I bless my good, and my life, more good manifests for me.

I know and firmly believe now that my greatest asset is my ability to choose my own thoughts. I choose only optimistic and positive thoughts about life and living from this moment on.

Whenever a negative thought enters my mind, I now catch it, and replace it with a positive one. Every day, I become more positive. Life is good.

Whenever a negative thought enters my mind, I immediately catch it and replace it with a positive thought.

I tell myself that "up until now" what I had been thinking might have been the truth, but it no longer is. I tell myself that from this moment on, I am making new choices for myself and only choosing what is best for me in my life.

I am maintaining my positive optimistic attitude about life and living. It is easy to do this because good, and, even more good is flooding into my life. I embrace it with open arms.

I now control of my own weight. I am in control of my mind and body. I am now choosing what I wish to take place in my world, mentally, emotionally, and physically.

I am now maintaining my ideal weight for the rest of my life.

I am taking off any unwanted weight easily and naturally.

My self - image is now one of me at my perfect weight. My new image of myself at my perfect weight helps me to control my eating behavior. I am happy. I am healthy. I am slim and healthy.

As a hypnotherapist, and metaphysician, approaches would be different. A hypnotherapist cannot treat medical problems without working with a physician. Licensed hypnotherapists can and do work with physicians.

You however can begin affirming that your body is functioning perfectly and normally with perfection. As many physicians in today s' world, I believe that changing our thoughts does in fact change our world.

As a licensed Practitioner, I could do treatments for you. This means that through my mind I see your wholeness and perfection, and through the power of Infinite Intelligence and your receptivity to a perfect healing, you are now an image of perfect health. You would experience the meditative state of mind, and accept your healing. You'll be amazed.

Use your self- hypnosis, and/or meditation each day to accept all the good that life has to offer. This includes perfect health in mind and body and in all of your affairs.

Remember that in your using affirmations to be calm, relaxed, and at peace, you are eliminating the eating which is done as a result of stress.

More and more doctors are acknowledging the body mind connection. They are now listening to their patients and getting clues of the thought processes that are causing problems.

Find the affirmation for building your self- esteem that are comfortable for you to use, and use them to break the compulsion type habits.

Use the up- until- now theory to break up any need to continue to hold yourself back or continue on with self-defeating behavior patterns.

"Up until now, I might have had a need to punish myself or hurt myself or others, but now, I am letting that go." "I am so busy improving myself, I no longer have any need or reason to be hurting myself by hurting others." I now treat others as I desire to be treated myself.

Being overweight is a complex problem.

It can stem from deep emotional beginnings to just having simple bad habits. It can be from identification with family or others. The symptom can be physical, mental, or emotional.

Here are just some of the reasons we become overweight. As you look down this list, check off any of the reasons that you might identify with. Next, you can write your own custom-designed affirmation to counterbalance that concept in your mind. Feel free to combine your affirmation with any of mine.

Compulsion to eat anything

Hungry every hour or two

Having a strong desire to eat sweets

Eat whether calm or happy

Eat when nervous

Nibble when watching television

Conscious or unconscious desire to remain unattractive to the opposite sex

Sexual frustration or guilt

Slow metabolism

Slow thyroid gland, or other glandular problem

Kidney problems, body holds too much fluid

High or low blood sugar

Masochism, a compulsion to hurt or punish your self

Sadism, a compulsion to punish others

Hypnosis, and hypnotherapy provide effective means of correcting weight problems because:

We work on achievement motivation and assure that it is established

Guilt feelings and diet rules are removed

Correct food selection is made easier

You become more goal oriented

When using tapes or going to a hypnotherapist, an interpersonal relationship is created

Emotional support is provided.

Remember to consult with your physician when embarking on a weight loss program. As you can see, there are physical problems that could be the cause of some of your weight.

I wish you the very best in your weight loss program.

Thank you for allowing me to be included in your program.

Catherine

Helpmates for you with
Special savings

Order your "**Change Eating Pattern**" cassette tape to aid you in your program now and receive a 50% discount off the purchase price.

Rather than working alone in the beginning, you can benefit and get results with help. When you

Listen to a cassette, you do nothing but kick back and relax. Let me do the work, as you reap the deep conditioning provided on this tape.

This is a relaxation tape that will reinforce your affirmations and assist you in achieving a deeper relaxation experience as you condition your self to use your self-hypnosis and meditation on your own.

This particular tape has helped thousands of students over the last twenty-seven years with excellent results. ***Order today, you will be glad you did!***

Order through losing weight feeling great.com

free

Full product catalog available on this website

or order Direct Catherine Elizabeth $15^{00} PO Box 2893 Nantucket Ma 02584

Another special offer for you

Losing Weight Feeling Great available on cassette/cd

Take the message and thoughts with you in your car or listen at your convenience at any time or place.

It is said that we need to hear something at least three times before we totally retain it. Repetition is effective and beneficial.

With this program, you will also receive a free cassette that is only affirmations. You may play these also in your car or anywhere to assist you in accepting your good.

You would never regret this purchase!

"Good News"

Visit losing weight feeling great.com

**The Companion Guide to this book is
Almost completed. Ask your
Local Bookstore or check with 1stBooks about
it's Availability. Coming Soon.
This is a special publication.
More info**

losing weight feeling great.com

"Ocean Experience- video"

Treat yourself to this wonderful experience. Imagine the most awesome ocean scenes beginning with a school of dolphins rising and sinking back into the sea. Throughout this video, there are scenes ranging from fast action of ocean waves to still serene scenes of the tide-pools in the rocks on the shore.

Several days of professional videotaping, are captured in this twenty- minute relaxation tape. We chose the most impressive scenes. Some have used this tape just as backdrop sounds in their living rooms when company arrives.

Throughout this video, there are affirmations that are spoken, as well as character generated on the screen. These affirmations are designed to heal ones soul and emotions. I threw in a few extras such as prosperity just to be well rounded.

This video has incredible healing and relaxation power. It ends with a wonderful sunset over the sea.

Special tapes and special reports

The "Transitions" tapes and cd's were created as a direct result of Catherine's popularity as a speaker, seminar leader and counselor. They have been revised over the 29 years in use.

On these tapes Catherine shares deep relaxation and motivational techniques integrated with affirmations that have helped thousands cope with today's fast paced life styles and stressful situations.

The Transitions special reports are short self-improvement reports that are a compliment to be read alone or in conjunction with the cassettes, or cd's.

Catherine's first book "Positive Power People," was co-authored with other members of the National Speakers Association. She was a member of that organization for 16 years. Her basic sincerity and genuine caring for people is reflected in her work.

Her children's books, "Positive Strokes for Little Folks" bring full circle her ability to relate to people of all ages.

The central message from Catherine is for you to go from where you are to where you want to be easily quickly and effortlessly.

As a licensed Practitioner with the Science of Mind church for 12 years, and, with a year of ministerial school, Ms. Wiands is a skilled metaphysician and she presents powerful and effective meditations. She had delivered sermons at Unity, Methodist and other churches nationwide.

Note: Our Transitions products are not intended as a substitute for a physician. If you need therapy or have a complex problem, please consult a physician.

Browse through the material below, and make your selections. You may order through our website, Nantucket Self Help Center.com

Starter tapes

Introduction to Relaxation
Side one explains self-hypnosis and how it will work for you. Side two is a relaxation exercise that you will find easy to do.

Affirmation Tape Pak

This special two-tape program is complete and easy to understand. It is a great place to start your relaxation experiences. Tape one; side one explains the theory of the mind. What is an affirmation? Where, why and how do you use affirmations to get results? Side two, is a relaxation exercise designed to crate the desire at a subconscious level to use affirmations in your everyday life, and to change negative restrictive behavior patterns you no longer want or need into positive ones.

Tape two is affirmations, affirmations and more affirmations. You may play this tape at any time, in any place and for many things. It has varied affirmation areas. You will love this concept. You can utilize it in your drive to work and set the tone for the whole day. You can use it while you travel. The places are endless. It is great! Over the years a favorite.

Advanced tape series

The Peaceful Room

Go to 1 Room, the peaceful room of your mind and find peace, serenity and understanding. Discover how wonderful you really are. Become aware. Treat yourself to this beautiful experience. Peaceful Room 2 is a shortened version for those wanting a ten-minute relaxation.

This tape is powerful. Results and benefits galore.

Develop Confidence

Improved confidence and a good self-image are the first steps in realizing your own marvelous potential. Learn to like yourself the way you really are.

Relax and sell

This tape presents a step-by-step procedure for presenting yourself and your product or service in a convincing manner by imagining a successful presentation. You know that you have a valuable product or service and that your clients are benefited by it. You make it become real. You will be amazed.

Oceans to Mountains.

This tape has to be heard to be appreciated. On one side you travel to the mountains and "Discover yourself." On the other side you go to the ocean where you let go of all the past hurt, anger, disappointment, and worry and begin to live again.

You meet the wise person and receive an answer to one of your personal questions about your life. Oceans to Mountains two is a shortened version of side one.

Stop Smoking

Are you an identification, or a substitution smoker? Do you really want to quit smoking? This is a pleasant and effective way to make it happen. Try it and see. Give our stop smoking tape a chance to work for you. You will be glad you did.

Improving Relationships

Because we believe relationships are so important to each of us, we are offering tape one of improving relationships as a single. Begin developing better understanding and enjoying more satisfying relationships... today!

Take Exams Easily

No matter what the subject situation or exam setting, this tape will assist you in taking exams with confidence and a positive attitude. You will enjoy exam opportunities because you are able and pleased to demonstrate your knowledge.

Eliminate Procrastination

One of the most popular tapes we have. As human beings, we have the tendency to put things off and make adjustments rather than to take action. This tape will help you develop a "do-it-now" attitude and you will watch things get done.

Sound Like a Winner

Public speaking becomes a natural and comfortable thing as you listen to this tape. Use it and develop real confidence in front of any audience large or small. You will have a flow in your presentation. You will have the ability to think on your feet and to answer questions extemporaneously. At times you will amaze your self. Try this one and see.

Healing Emotions

Many of us have old hurts and pain mixed with sadness. This tape was created to heal those old wounds and allow you to move forward without all the sadness and sorrow.

Where Has the Happiness Gone?

Learn to become a more contented person. Develop a new awareness about yourself that others can't help to see. You take on a new glow and enthusiasm. Make the decision to bring happiness back into your life. If you cant remember being happy, this tape will guide you.

Living with a Negative Person

Learn a method which can control the effects negative people and things have on you. Remember that it takes 15-18 positive statements to yourself for every negative one you have accepted from others, or even given yourself. You will see and feel results, as you use other's negativity as a catalyst for your peace of mind and success.

Concentration

Learn to develop single mindedness and focus. Learn to use the power within you to concentrate well. This enhances your relaxation process as well. This is an important skill to have in any and all walks of life.

Memory

Another important key to success is a good memory. If you have trouble with facts, names, dates, places etc. this tape is the one for you. We all have a wonderful memory; we just need to redevelop it.

Creative Mental Vacations

Various creative visualizations to stimulate your imagination meditate and get away from it all This product presents different locations and styles of deepening the relaxation process.

Surfside treasures

This is one of our most popular meditations. Listen to the sea, as you allow all of your good be accepted into mind. Spaces of silence are provided for your private thoughts. This is powerful.

Power within

Allow your personal power to surface and be utilized in all areas of your life. The power is there, all you need to do is tap into it.

Improve your Physical Skills

It doesn't matter what sport or activity you are involved in, you can see tremendous improvement with the use of this tape. Discover the awesome power of your mind, while at the same time, reaping added benefits of relaxation, and results.

Healing codependency

This is a two tape program (one cd) which provides healing techniques for healing codependent behaviors and the pain which has resulted from being codependent. This program discusses the dynamics of codependency, and how to overcome them.

Freedom from the hidden addiction-gambling

What makes people gamble? What are the differences between male and female gamblers?

Break the cycle of this destructive behavior.

Stop the pain which results from this habit.

Take control over your life and your destiny.

Do it now.

True story of a walk back to wholeness having survived a destruction and abusive relationship. Catherine shares her story. This is a fast-moving, thought provoking story, encompassing 18 years in an abusive and violent marriage and the depression it created. New awareness of codependent behaviors and how they manifest are blended with humor, you will find this work hard to put down.

This book is written from the heart and it provides insight and benefits galore. Self help strategies are woven throughout in a creative and effective fashion. Catherine will speak to any group on these issues regarding her walk from national speaker, author seminar leader torn complete down with the incestuous components in this type of relationship and she will provide information and knowledge to walk back into the mainstream of life.

As listeners and Readers learn how the wrong relationship can tear down the most dynamic people and the walk back to wholeness although challenging at times can be made!

"Unveiled Deception" by Catherine Elizabeth

New Book. Self Hypnosis works (for every little thing)

Check our website losing weight feeling great.com

ABOUT THE AUTHOR

Catherine loves presenting her "no nonsense, no frills, just basic principles that work" programs. Her love of her work, and sense of humor is reflected in each presentation. She is a seasoned speaker, seminar leader and workshop facilitator with twenty-six years experience.

Ms. Annett became a licensed hypnotherapist in California. She opened her business, Changing Attitudes in La Jolla. In eighteen, months she went from recluse to having international clientele. She was named in *Who's Who among San Diego Women* two years running.

Marriage brought her to Arizona where she completed her licensed practitioner certification. For ten years she presented both her programs as well as sermons, speeches, personal sessions, meditations and attended ministerial school.

She was published in magazines, newspapers, worked in television and radio, and hosted her own show, "What Happens to the Children," co authored *Positive Power People*, while teaching and producing her own twenty-seven self-help tapes, guides, the "Ocean Experience Video," and *Positive Strokes for Little Folks* books and cassette.

Her students are from all walks of life and all ages from corporate, to colleges, the government, and the private sector.

Now residing in Nantucket, Massachusetts, she has completed this book by popular demand.

Printed in the United States
25649LVS00003B/503